A Learning Ideabook™

Trash Artists Workshop

by Linda Allison

Fearon Teacher Aids, a division of PITMAN LEARNING, INC. Belmont, California

The author wishes to thank Peter Pfaelzer for his creative help, and Susan Straight and Cheryl Crecelious for their classroom expertise.

OTHER TITLES IN THE CRAFTS WORKSHOP SERIES:

INVENTORS WORKSHOP
MAKE YOUR OWN GAMES WORKSHOP
NATIVE AMERICAN CRAFTS WORKSHOP
NATURE CRAFTS WORKSHOP

Editorial director: Roberta Suid
Editor: Bonnie Bernstein
Production editor: Mary McClellan
Design manager: Eleanor Mennick
Designer: Jane Mitchell
Illustrator: Linda Allison
Cover designer: William Nagel

ISBN–0–8224–9780–8
Library of Congress Card Catalog Number: 80–84184
Printed in the United States of America.

1 9 8 7 6 5 4 3 2 1

Preface

Newspapers can be melted into a modeling compound.

Boxes can take flight as boomerangs.

Billboard art can be folded into long books.

A pile of old clothes can rise again and take on an uncanny presence as a life-sized rag person.

Styrofoam scraps can stamp up a storm of designs or sail across a pond as seaworthy ships.

Brown bags, bubble-top bottles, plastic lids, and lollipop sticks can all be art supplies if you are in the right frame of mind. This is something that a lot of artists, such as Picasso, have known for a long time. And it's something kids catch on to pretty fast. One of the things kids like best about throwaway materials is that they can experiment and use them in a free-spirited way. After all, if an idea doesn't succeed, they can always throw it back in the trash.

Trash Artists Workshop contains a series of projects and recipes that use all sorts of junk, odds and ends, fractured bits and pieces, and throwaways as the material for a wide range of artworks. Some of the ideas are old classics — such as sawdust clay, a modeling compound that every art teacher on a tight budget should know about. Other ideas are as new as a bubble-top deodorant bottle made into an outsized marker. All of them require a minimum of store-bought supplies. Each project has been road-tested for success with kids and chosen with a certain quality in mind. Just because you start with trash doesn't mean you have to finish with trash. Trash, like any other material, deserves a little respect. That's why teaching kids care and pride in their work is part of the aim of this book. Consider the Watts Towers, a monumental sculpture that has survived vandals, city bureaucrats, and earthquakes. It may be built of trash, but it's made to last.

In addition to over 50 crafts projects, **Trash Artists Workshop** features tales of inspiration — examples of legendary trash art and trash artists. There is a list of resources for those who want more on trash art and The Trash Artist's Guide to Trash for those who want some little hints on how to ferret out more unusual sources of throwaways.

Individual projects are written so that kids can read them and make the items independently or with a minimum of adult supervision. **Trash Artists Workshop** is geared to both you and the kids you are working with. You can start anywhere, but a good place to dig in and begin is in the first chapter, Introducing the Trash Artist, which features several creativity exercises.

Trash art demands an active imagination to transform a piece of junk into something wonderful. That's why, more than an arts and crafts book, this is a book about seeing old things in new ways. It's about breaking out of the conventional ways of thinking. It's about encouraging the imagination and building skills in creativity. It's about using the ordinary in an extraordinary way.

Contents

Introduction

Introducing the Trash Artist

In 1913 Marcel Duchamp made a sculpture that caused an uproar. It was called *Bicycle Wheel.* It was exactly that, a bike wheel mounted on an old kitchen stool. But was it art?

Duchamp said it was non-sculpture. He showed other pieces of "ready-made" art, such as a hat rack hanging from the ceiling, a urinal, and a bottle holder. According to him, it was all art. The critics called it trash.

About the same time, artists like Pablo Picasso and Georges Braque began making pictures from bits of scrap, using a technique called collage. Letters from newspapers, swatches of chair caning, lengths of rope—the artist pasted them all onto canvas and painted or drew over them to make a picture. The critics didn't like these either. More trash, they said. No wonder they didn't like it. It was a rejection of an art tradition—a tradition which dictated that artists use fine paint or marble as the medium for creations which must be made to look like the real world.

This use of junk made people look at real world objects in a new way. By putting a frame around throwaway materials, it forced people to take a careful look at everyday things, to notice that there might be beauty in the trash. These artists said that art was an act of imagination, not paint applied prettily to a canvas. They rejected the idea that an artist had to draw or carve. They experimented with new techniques and materials, and created pictures and sculpture from ordinary, everyday stuff. Their art was strange and different—and very imaginative.

If that wasn't enough rule-breaking, trash artists began making art that moved. Sometimes it even made noises while it moved. One of the most famous of the "kinetic" sculptures, or sculptures in motion, was made by Jean Tinguely in the 1960s. He created a machine called *Homage to New York,* which included a piano, wheels, belts, pulleys, a bathtub, and 15 motors. Altogether it contained more than 400 junk parts. This machine was built to self-destruct at an event at the Museum of Modern Art. Tinguely took the controls and started the machine. Parts began to hum, shake, spin, sputter, and whine. Then, in a moment of glory, *Homage* caught fire and was extinguished forever by the New York City Fire Department.

Other artists have carried on the trash tradition, under different labels. Junk art has gone by names like collage, assemblage, kinetic sculpture, and Dada. Artists like Joseph Cornell, Max Ernst, Kurt Schwitters, Mark di Suvero, John Chamberlain, Louise Nevelson, and Robert Rauschenberg have all built their reputations transforming junk into art.

Therefore, as a teacher of young, aspiring trash artists, you are following in the tradition of some of the greats. And the path to success is relatively unlittered with material problems such as money and availability of supplies. But you may run into some attitude debris.

THE MUD FLATS

If you ever drive to San Francisco across the Bay Bridge, you are sure to see the Emeryville mud flats. Actually you won't notice the mud flats as much as you will notice the amazing collection of wooden people, fish, castles, and monsters that rise out of them. These works of art have appeared in magazines, on postcards, and in films. The interesting thing about this majestic sculpture garden is that it is built entirely from junk. The currents and tides make the mud flats a collection spot for all sorts of flotsam and jetsam that float on the bay. The area is thick with a rich assortment of wood, tin cans, old shoes, plastic bottles, and rubber tires.

Once somebody braved the mud and the rich smells and waded out on the flats. When this anonymous artist left, a trash sculpture stood to greet the commuters that drive into the city on the freeway. Then someone built another sculpture to keep company with the first. The idea caught on. More appeared. Ten or fifteen years later, folks still bring their imaginations, hammers, and a handful of nails to erect sphinxes, trains, wooden Indians, flying fish, and signs, such as "Happy Birthday Wanda," right on the spot. The show is ever-changing. Pieces become weather-beaten and die, or get cannibalized for other works. No artists get credit. The most they get out of it is a sense of satisfaction that comes from transforming junk into art and a whole lot of smiles from those folks on the freeway.

How do you get kids to share your enthusiasm? How do you find a way to see the vast number of possibilities in a stack of newspapers or a Styrofoam cup? The rest of this introduction addresses itself to these sorts of questions.

GOOD CLEAN FUN

There I was at the mud flats, ankle-deep in a smorgasbord of trash with a bunch of bright, enthusiastic, creative kids. It was a nice day; we had hammer, nails, and no lack of imagination. I, for one, was ready to build a junk sculpture to remember.

The problem was that they weren't. These kids thought all that trash was disgusting. They minced around. They made faces at the mud on their shoes and complained about the smells. They had serious doubts about whether they should have come at all and made a lot of comments about germs and cooties.

What a bunch of turkeys, I thought. Why didn't I bring some good kids? I wondered with exasperation. I had forgotten that children can be some of the most conservative people on earth. Kids don't necessarily leap at the chance to try something new, especially if it smells. Kids like to be safe and cool. Trash is neither.

A lot of adults are under the erroneous impression that kids are naturally creative in all circumstances. They can be, but given the choice, they will reach for clean paper and nice, whole crayons. After all, you probably have spent a lot of time drumming into them the idea that litter is loathsome. Just because *you* see the possibilities in trash art doesn't mean that your young artist friends will.

It's up to you to change their minds. One of the best ways to do this is to show them something you've constructed from this book, such as a terrific warrior **Jug Head** mask. Give them a chance to get excited about the project. When you tell them it's made from half of an old bleach bottle, they'll come to their own conclusion that being a trash artist is perfectly respectable, not to mention the fact that it can be a whole lot of fun.

Some trash art projects will lend themselves to a structured way of working; others will be more open-ended. Don't worry about snuffing out creativity by involving kids in a structured project. Kids are bound to make whatever they attempt an individualistic effort by the way they hold those scissors and push a paintbrush around. Children have a way of coming through with the most inventive variations.

On the other hand, don't be afraid to embark on a process-oriented project, like gluing together a wood scrap sculpture, where there is no specific model or goal. The finished product is not as important as the journey or the side trips of discovery along the way. You should get the kids started, then move aside. Sometimes you will want to offer advice and direct the outcome. Don't do it. Stand by to offer encouragement and enthusiasm. Every artist needs an audience. Keep tuned. Often really wonderful variations on ideas turn up. Note these for future reference. And remember, trash art is good, clean fun. Your kids will catch on.

THE WATTS TOWERS

One of the most famous monuments to junk art is the Watts Towers. This fanciful collection of spires, arches, and fountains rises unexpectedly from the backyard of a perfectly ordinary house in a perfectly ordinary neighborhood in Los Angeles. The towers rise more than a hundred feet into the air and are built from junk materials. Steel rod and iron mesh are covered with bits of tile, broken china, pieces of mirrors, bottles, and seashells.

Simon Rodia began this project in 1920 and worked piecing his towers together bit by bit for 33 years. He worked without help except for the kids in the neighborhood who would sometimes bring him junk materials. He paid them in cookies and pennies.

In 1954 Simon gave the deed to the land to his neighbor and disappeared. Despite neglect, earthquakes, and the city's attempts to get them torn down, Simon Rodia's towers still stand. In fact, this monumental collection of junk has become a national landmark visited by more than 25,000 people every year.

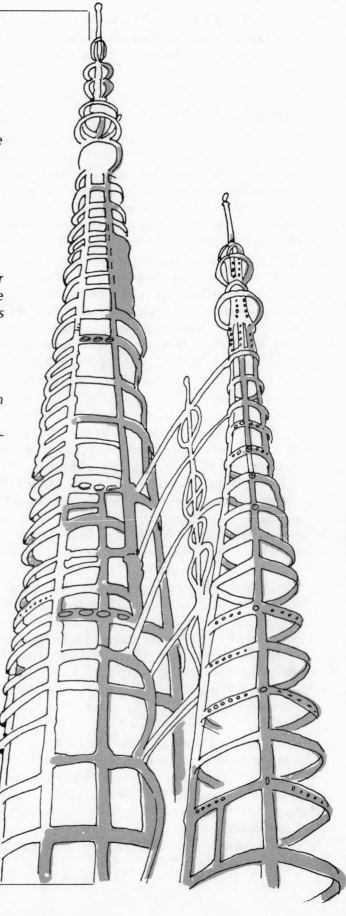

THE EGG CARTON PROBLEM

Some things just seem like trash. To me, egg cartons are one of those things. No matter what you do to them, they look better in the garbage. Paint them, cut them, stick on pipe cleaner antennas—they still look like egg cartons that have been tampered with.

However, they are an easy find and a plentiful, free material. It seemed my duty while writing this book to figure out a way to turn egg cartons into something wonderful. There *had* to be something a person could do with them.

I took my problem to my friend Peter who is in the business of teaching people to be creative. He diagnosed my problem with egg cartons as prejudice and a creative block. "This calls for some creative problem solving," he said. "Why don't we make an attribute list?"

"Okay," I agreed.

We wrote down everything that distinguished an egg carton—things like purple, lightweight, floatable, modular, stackable, and biodegradable. Suggestions began popping up from the list of attributes: Depressions—how about a starter for seeds? Raised places—a ring toss game? Repetitive pattern—wallpaper? Peter saw a raccoon face. I thought of little masks. Egg cartons would make great bulging eyes.

That's how the idea for making **Half Masks** came about—an idea that changed my mind about the possibilities in an egg carton.

CREATIVITY EXERCISES

You may find that you and your kids also need to fight some preconceptions and flex those inventive mental muscles in order to overcome creative blocks. So, here are four creativity exercises designed to help you avoid the egg carton syndrome. Use them yourself to come up with new and original trash art projects. Use them with kids to stimulate their imaginations and encourage their creative thinking.

Brainstorming. Brainstorming is a collective activity that helps kids to free their imaginations. Include everybody around in your brainstorming sessions. First think of a problem that needs a solution. Present the problem to your kids and ask them to come up with as many solutions as they can. Provide some rules and guidelines before the session formally begins. Every player has to talk first and think later—even the shy ones. Judging ideas is no fair. The wilder the ideas are, the better. There are no turns, so you might want to appoint more than one scribe to be sure that every idea gets recorded.

Here's a sample problem: Think of twelve tiny presents to give on the twelve days of Christmas, each small enough to fit into one of the twelve cups of an egg carton.

Here are some solutions: small shells, twelve different kinds of gum balls wrapped in gold foil, a dozen haiku poems, little works of art, a rock collection, an emerald (remember, no fair being practical), a pressed flower, paper clips, a tiny green frog, twelve chocolate-covered cherries, a lock of hair, a key to your heart.

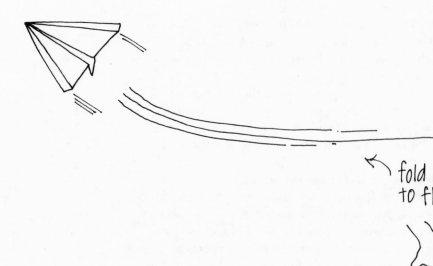

When the list is quite long, it's time to judge the ideas that have come out of your brainstorming session. Of course, some of them will be terribly impractical, but one kid's craziest idea can often be a stepping-stone to the best idea any of you ever had.

Verb It. Remind kids that verbs are words that show action or change. Verbs are good for putting kids' imaginations to work changing how they think about things.

Make your kids a proposition. Tell them you're going to change the way they think about something with a bunch of action verbs. For instance, have them consider those little plastic clasps that hold shut bags of bread. What on earth could you do with them? Ask them to apply the verbs on the list to the clasp and see what possibilities they can imagine.

Magnify: Make the clasp bigger. What if it closed a giant bag of bread? What if it were a bib or a dinner plate with a hole to hold a cup?

Multiply: Two of them could be earrings. A handful would make a necklace of flower petals, or confetti at a wedding. Any number could be used to decorate a Christmas tree.

Reverse: Turn it upside down or backwards. It could be an opener instead of a closer, a knife, or a scraper—one idea usually leads to another.

Shrink: It's sand on an artificial beach.

Combine: Add it to something. Put a bunch of clasps in a jar and shake it like a maraca. Clip them together to make a chain, a belt, or a dog collar.

Adapt: What if it had a bigger hole? You could wear it as a ring. What if it were soft? You get the idea.

Attribute List. This is a simple strategy to help kids see something as it really is, as a composite of all its features, rather than simply a label. Have each child pick a thing and make a list of its qualities. The list should be long—as many as 50 attributes. You might have the kids study themselves for starters. What are their attributes—size, color, likes, and dislikes? Ask: What do people like about you? What are you good at? What are you bad at? After the list reaches 50, a kid should have a pretty good idea about what a thing *really* is and should see well past its label.

Newspaper Anything. Here is a way to test creative power with a common, everyday material any kid can find around the house. What's black and white and read all over, makes great costumes, wraps up garbage, and folds up into hats, shoes, or planters?

Provide the kids with a newspaper, string, tape, and a pair of scissors. Have them experiment with what newspaper will do when they crush it, crinkle it, roll it, curl it, tear it, shred it, stack it, and fold it. Then ask them to think, How would I make newspaper shoes? How would I make a planter, a flyswatter, an air conditioner, a chair, a clock, a back scratcher, or a place to hide out? When someone has figured out a way, tell him or her to go ahead and do it!

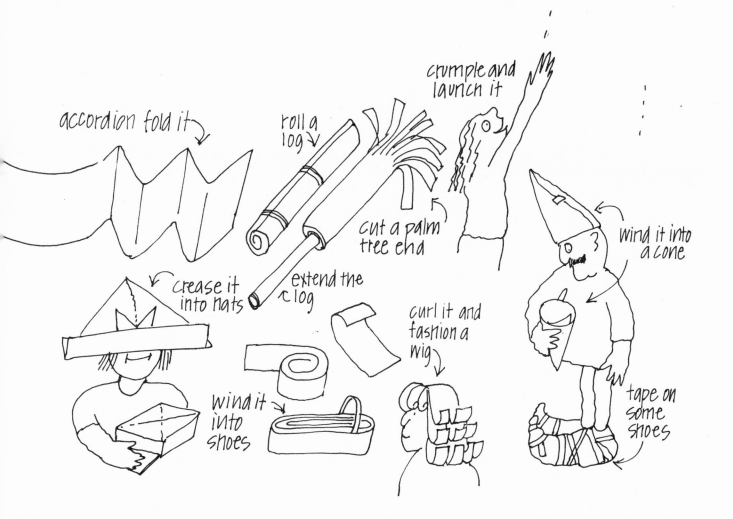

accordion fold it

roll a log

crumple and launch it

cut a palm tree end

wind it into a cone

crease it into hats

extend the log

curl it and fashion a wig

wind it into shoes

tape on some shoes

The Trash Collector

Collecting the Trash

There are many different ways to collect trash. Teachers or group leaders can send an all-purpose list home with the kids to let parents know which discards to save for art projects. There is a list of wanted throwaways ready to photocopy and send home at the end of this chapter (see page 12).

If you have a very cooperative group of parents, you are likely to have a steady supply of materials. But not all teachers are so lucky. You might want to arrange with other teachers to pool your trash collection and store it in the art supply room. An alternative is to collect materials as you need them. A few weeks before a project, leave a container at a collection point. For instance, if you are in need of Styrofoam cups, leave a note by the coffee machine in the teachers' lounge. Or leave a note and a box near the trash basket in the home economics classroom requesting fabric scraps.

For parents working with kids, or kids working by themselves, there are some ideas for collecting, organizing, and storing material in **The Trash Artist's Studio** (see Chapter 3, page 16). It is also possible to leave notes and boxes at collection points, such as the trash bin at your apartment building to request magazines, or the photocopy machine in an office to request those wonderfully sturdy cardboard cylinders from empty rolls of mimeograph paper.

Don't be afraid to do a little soliciting. Ask yourself, Who uses big pieces of cardboard? Who gets rid of old burlap sacks? Then check the yellow pages and phone the appropriate business or industry and ask for their scraps. They are usually only too delighted to give you some of their trash.

For those who are new at using trash as an art medium—and for those old pros who are always on the lookout for new sources of art supplies—on the next page you will find **The Trash Artist's Guide to Trash,** or who throws away what.

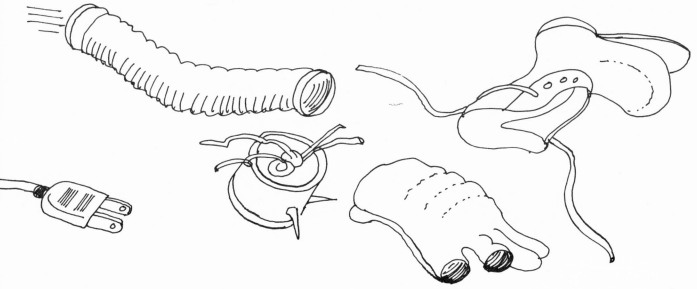

The Trash Artist's Guide to Trash

APPLIANCE REPAIR SHOPS. Unclaimed clocks, radios, fans, and old parts are good for collage projects. An old television with the workings removed makes a good theater for finger puppets.

BILLBOARD COMPANIES. Gigantic pieces of billboard paper, white on one side and printed in color on the other, are great for any large art project.

BOWLING ALLEYS. Did you know that bowling alleys throw away their old and damaged bowling pins? Ask the manager to save you some if you can figure out how to use them.

CABINET SHOPS. The best sources for classy wood scraps, sawdust, and wood curls are cabinetmakers. Ask them to save you a boxful.

CANNED FOOD STORES. The supermarkets that sell items right out of the carton always have a ready supply of boxes.

CARPET STORES. Some carpet stores occasionally give away old sample books.

CONSTRUCTION SITES. Lumber scraps, pipes, molding, tile scraps, electrical wire, and bits of hardware are available with a little scrounging around construction sites. Make friends with the builders. Expect to find different materials at various points in the construction. But ask permission to scrounge first. The sites are private property and you don't want to trespass.

DELICATESSENS. Ask for wooden crates and boxes that hold cheese. Some of the larger ones are quite elegant.

DEPARTMENT STORES. Periodically request stock boxes, carpet samples, plastic bags, wire hangers, big boxes, all sorts of packing materials, old signs, and displays. Don't ask for everything at once!

ELECTRONIC STORES. Electronic equipment comes shipped in fascinating assortments of Styrofoam containers. Ask for these at any store that sells appliances, such as hardware, department, or drug stores. Also ask for empty wire spools.

FABRIC STORES. Fabric boards (the ones yardage is wrapped around) are good for collages. Sometimes pattern books and fabric scraps are also available.

FAST FOOD RESTAURANTS. Plastic straws, Styrofoam boxes, paper napkins, cups, and other disposables can be salvaged from fast food places.

FLOUR MILLS. If you happen to find one of these in the phone book, give them a call. They sometimes give away bolt ends of sack material, a great source of new cloth with interesting printing.

FURNITURE AND APPLIANCE STORES. Enormous boxes that contain refrigerators or other large appliances can be cut into a theater for puppet shows. They are a good source for big sheets of cardboard.

FURNITURE FACTORIES. Ask for scrap wood, foam, and fabric pieces.

FOOD MARKETS. Crates, boxes, mesh bags, plastic lids, packing materials, and discarded display racks may be out back by the dumpster.

HARDWARE STORES. Color swatches, wood scraps for free or cheap, tile, and wallpaper samples may be yours for the asking.

ICE CREAM PARLORS. Three- and five-gallon round cartons are good for storage.

LIQUOR STORES. Ask for cigar boxes here and at tobacco shops. Cardboard boxes with dividers, the kind that jug wine bottles are shipped in, make an instant, organized storage system.

LUMBERYARDS. Most lumberyards will let you take home bags of sawdust or wood shavings for free. Another great find is formica sink cutouts which make smooth, practically indestructible, desk-size work surfaces. If they're not free, they'll be very cheap.

NEWSPAPERS. Ask your local press for their newsprint paper roll ends. These yield sheets of paper about 30 inches wide and a few hundred feet long. Draw your heart out, make costumes, or cover a picnic table.

PHOTO STUDIOS. Collect film cans and canisters in plastic and metal. Ask for the sturdy, black-lined boxes that photo printing paper comes in. They are good for frames and storage. Some are quite large.

PICTURE FRAMERS. Some framing shops give away the center cut-out sections of mats. Mat factories also give away ovals and round boards. This is very high-class art material.

PLASTIC COMPANIES. Trimmings of tubes, pipes, and scraps of plastic sheets are trash to them, great finds to you.

PRINTING COMPANIES. Scraps of paper in all colors, sizes, and weights are thrown away by printers. Sometimes printers will give away boxes that reams of standard size paper are shipped in — perfect for files. If there's a paper-punch drill, you may be able to take home a bag of colorful confetti.

RESTAURANTS. Here's a wonderful source of big, beautiful tin cans. The five-gallon oil tins make good storage bins when they're cleaned and the tops are removed. Egg flats, asparagus boxes, and crates may also be on hand.

SAIL MAKERS AND SLEEPING BAG MANUFACTURERS. Scraps of colorful, rip-stop nylon and stuffing scraps have all sorts of potential.

SELF-SERVICE LAUNDRIES. Periodically check a local coin laundry for bleach bottles, cardboard soap boxes, and stray socks for stuffed animals.

SCHOOLS. What does your school throw away? Milk cartons? Food trays? Scrap paper office forms (clean on one side)? Some schools have a stash of discarded books which are collages waiting to happen.

SHOE STORES. Sometimes shoe boxes can be had in sets of 12, all in a larger box. Shoe boxes make instant file cabinets or art supply drawers.

SHOE, BELT, AND HANDBAG FACTORIES, AND LEATHER REPAIR SHOPS. Check the phone book under *leather*. Give each place a call and ask for leather scraps.

TELEPHONE COMPANIES. Ask the phone company's maintenance department for scraps of wire. The wire they use is covered in bright-colored plastic. While you're at it, request old phones and wooden wire spools.

TURKEY RANCHES AND CHICKEN FARMS. Poultry farms are your best bet for wonderful collections of feathers.

UPHOLSTERY AND TAILOR SHOPS. Foam and fabric scraps, buttons, spools, cord, and trims are always lying around upholstery and tailor shops. Ask for them.

Wanted: Your Throwaways

Dear _____,

   Our class will be doing art projects using recycled materials. We need your help. Please save and send any of the following to school in *clean* condition. Many thanks.

BUTTONS	FABRIC SCRAPS
JUNK MAIL	RUSTY METAL
STYROFOAM CUPS, LIDS	OLD CLOTHES, HATS, ACCESSORIES
EMPTY ROLL-ON DEODORANT BOTTLES	OLD SHEETS
PENCIL STUBS	PLASTIC STRAWS
BROOMSTICKS	YARN SCRAPS
SAWDUST	CHOP STICKS
CORKS	CURTAIN RODS
TOMATO OR BERRY BASKETS	MAGAZINES, COMIC BOOKS
SPOOLS	OIL PAINT
BOTTLETOPS	PAPER SCRAP (GIFT WRAPS, FOIL RIBBONS, MAPS)
STYROBOXES, MEAT TRAYS	
COAT HANGERS	CARDBOARD FROM BOXES, SHIRTBOARDS, TABLET BACKS
BROKEN CLOCKS	
MILK CARTONS	NEWSPAPERS
TIN CANS	STRING
BROKEN CRAYONS	PLASTIC CONTAINERS, LIDS
OLD TOOTHBRUSHES	PLASTIC SQUEEZE BOTTLES
NAILS	PLASTIC JUGS
ALUMINUM TINS	STYROFOAM CHUNKS, SHEETS
METAL BAND-AID BOXES	OLD WINDOWS, MIRRORS
MATCH BOXES	INCOMPLETE DECKS OF CARDS
CARDBOARD TUBES	PAPER BAGS
OATMEAL CONTAINERS	EGGSHELLS
BABY FOOD JARS	EGG CARTONS

S.C.R.A.P.

Did you ever need a roll of plastic? Or a box of ceramic tiles? Or a pound of leather scraps? Or yards of yarn? Bones? Old bike parts? Palm fronds? Plastic tubes? Plexiglas? Chicken wire? Cans? Chemicals? Spools? Cones? Old theater sets? Costumes? A bale of shredded gum wrappers? If you're lucky enough to live near San Francisco, you can get all that and more at an amazing place called S.C.R.A.P., which is short for Scrounger's Center for Reusable Art Parts. This trash artist's dream come true is located in a big warehouse in the industrial neighborhood of San Francisco.

S.C.R.A.P. is in the business of collecting industrial throwaways and making them available to artists and various community organizations, such as scouts, theater groups, and schools. The project started with nothing more than an idea and three paid salaries that were funded from grants. The people were hired, and three energetic workers dug right in and proceeded to scrounge an office, a phone, a truck, a space in a warehouse, and tons of throwaway materials from local industries.

They have been going strong for several years and are now funded by federal arts money and CETA grants. Besides providing free art materials, S.C.R.A.P.'s recycling saves the state considerable problems of disposal at landfill sites, which qualifies S.C.R.A.P. for money from California's State Solid Waste Management Board. Most of the materials would otherwise be hauled to the dump. S.C.R.A.P. also enjoys the support of local industries, who are delighted to be saved the time and expense of having to dump their throwaways. Besides, businesses get a bonus of a tax deduction for their contributions. S.C.R.A.P. is a good deal all around.

THE RECYCLE CENTER

East coast teachers and artists have their own wonderful depot of industrial scrap materials. It's called the Recycle Center, and it's housed in the Teacher Resource Center of the Boston Children's Museum.

In 1971 Elaine Gurian hired Leonard Gottlieb for the job of scrounger. His job was to fill a space she had designed with junk — reusable junk. Elaine had the backing of the Institute of Contemporary Art, in Boston, which liked her idea of making a warehouse where scrap materials could be collected and then distributed to anyone who wanted to use them.

Lenny turned out to be a talented scrounger. Factories began donating things like shoe buckles, old Navy maps, camera lenses, cardboard cutouts, and leather scraps. The customers began coming to buy bagfuls of scrap materials. Six months later they moved from the warehouse to the Boston Children's Museum, which gave them a larger space and more visibility. They called the place the Recycle Museum, or Recycle for short.

Recycle is still in business. There are tons and tons of scrap materials in the storage area. Shoppers don't see all of the materials. They visit a well-ordered room that has bins and bins of materials sorted according to kind. People describe this room as looking like a candy store with junk. They pick up a shopping bag and move through the bins selecting the stuff that they need. They pay a small fee for the materials. Big time users buy a membership in the operation.

One secret to Recycle's success is that, besides being in the junk business, they are in the idea business. This departure came in answer to the cry, "Great stuff, but what can I do with it?" Recycle responded by giving a series of workshops for teachers and kids and producing a collection of idea sheets for using their materials. The ideas have recently appeared as a collection in a book entitled Recyclopedia, *a compilation of games, science equipment, and crafts projects using recycled materials.*

Adapted from *Recyclopedia*, Robin Simons, Houghton Mifflin, 1976.

The Trash Artist's Studio

Cardboard Easel

Trash finds make not only good art materials, they can make a good art studio. There are many ways to turn trash into work surfaces and tools for art projects. To start with, here's a simple, corrugated cardboard easel.

MATERIALS

Corrugated cardboard (36 inches by 20 inches)
Tape (Any strong tape will do.)
Paper
Pushpins

TOOLS

Mat knife
Straight edge (A yardstick will work.)

HERE'S HOW

1. Draw the outline for the easel onto the cardboard.
2. Cut around the outside edge.
3. Score the cardboard along the dotted lines.
4. Bend the cardboard along the scored lines.
5. Fold up the flaps and tape them into position.
6. Slide the back into position.
7. Attach a sheet of paper to the easel with a pair of pushpins.
8. Set the easel on a table and paint away.

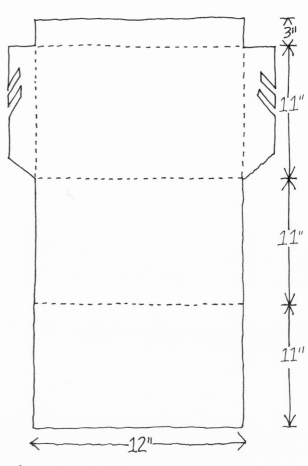

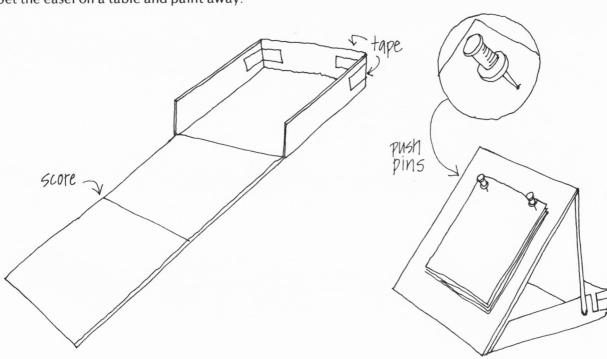

Newspaper Aprons

There will be times when trash artists will want some protection before starting an art project. Here is an apron that is cheap and fast to make. And it has the talent for keeping itself clean. When it gets dirty, just tear off the top layer to reveal a nice, neat one underneath and toss the grubby one in the trash.

MATERIALS

A section of the newspaper (about 20 pages)
Fat string or yarn (Use four 2-foot lengths. See **T-Shirt Yarn,** page 21.)

TOOLS

Paper punch
Scissors

HERE'S HOW

1. Open up the newspaper section. Remove any single page inserts. Tidy up the stack so that the edges are even.
2. Cut away the armhole sections as shown. Some adjusting may be necessary in order to get a good fit.
3. Punch four holes: two for the neck ties and two for the back ties.
4. Knot the ends of the strings to hold them in position. Thread the strings through the holes from front to back.
5. Tie on your apron.

Notes: This makes an apron for a big kid or an adult. A smaller version can be cut from a stack of half-sized sheets. Don't wear these aprons over light-colored clothing. Printer's ink has a way of rubbing off—especially if the ink is fresh.

Free-Flowing Newsprint

A newspaper office that uses a web printing press can be a source of yards and yards of free, clean-white newsprint paper. Phone the newspaper office and find out if they give away the ends of rolls of newsprint. This paper can be a bit unwieldy. Here is a solution that should make the big sheets of paper easy to use and store.

MATERIALS

Roll of newsprint
Broomstick
Rope

TOOLS

Large hook or nail
Small saw
Scissors
Straight edge (A yardstick will work.)

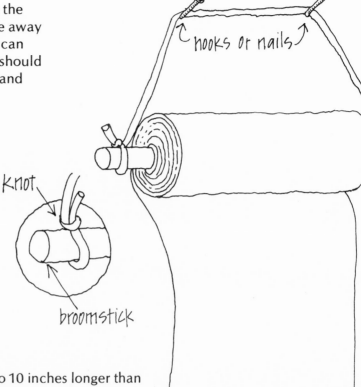

hooks or nails

Knot

broomstick

HERE'S HOW

1. Saw off the broomstick so that it is 6 to 10 inches longer than the width of the paper.
2. Cut a length of rope twice the length of the broomstick.
3. Slide the paper roll onto the broomstick.
4. Knot the ends of the rope to either end of the broomstick.
5. Suspend the newsprint holder from a hook or nail.
6. Hang a yardstick or some other straight edge nearby. Use it as a guide for tearing off sheets.

Notes: This makes an apron for a big kid or an adult. A smaller version can be cut from a stack of half-sized sheets. Don't wear these aprons over light-colored clothing. Printer's ink has a way of rubbing off—especially if the ink is fresh.

ruler

Roll-On Markers

The perfect companion to a roll of newsprint is a set of big, roll-on markers. Empty roll-on deodorant bottles can be uncapped, filled with paint, and lead whole new lives as giant pens. Don't expect them to draw as smoothly as felt markers. But they are good for big, bold drawings. And they are cheap and refillable.

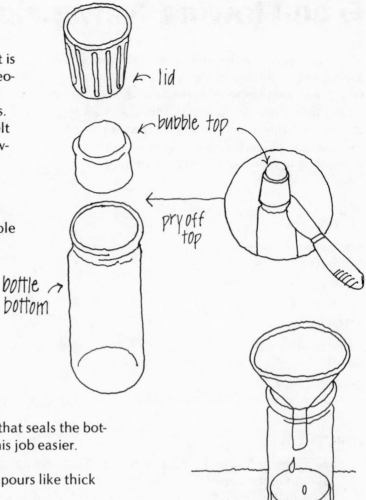

MATERIALS

Assorted roll-on bottles (the kind with a bubble applicator)
Poster paint
Water

TOOLS

Funnel
Table knife

HERE'S HOW

1. Take the bottle apart. Pry off the bubble that seals the bottle. The edge of a table knife will make this job easier.
2. Wash all the parts.
3. Dilute the poster paint with water until it pours like thick cream.
4. Fill the bottle with paint through a funnel.
5. Snap on the bubble and write away.

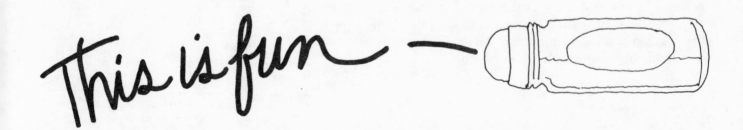

Note: Don't forget to screw on the top when the marker's not in use.

T-Shirt Yarn

This fat, colorful string has a million different uses. It makes a stout cord for binding up packages. It is good-looking enough to use to tie up a gift. And it's strong enough to tie up the dog. Use it in weaving projects around the classroom or any project that calls for wide, sassy yarn.

MATERIALS

Old T-shirts (The best kind to use are ones that have no side seams, but the other kind will work. Look for the ones that are single knit. Double-knit shirts won't curl into yarn.)

TOOLS

Scissors

HERE'S HOW

1. Trim off the hem of the T-shirt.
2. Carefully remove the pockets if there are any.
3. Cut into the bottom of the T-shirt at an angle. Snip off a strip about an inch wide. Cut all around the body of the T-shirt in a spiral, making a continuous, long strip.
4. Stretch the strip so that the edges curl under, making a fat yarn.
5. Wind the T-Shirt Yarn into balls.

remove hem and pocket

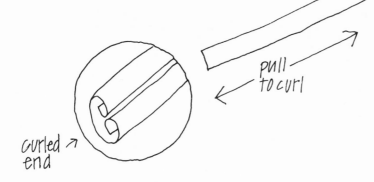

pull to curl

curled end

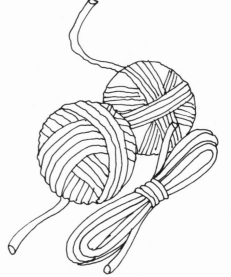

Notes: Garage sales are the cheapest source of old T-shirts if you can't get donations. Worn, faded, ratty-looking T-shirts will color right up with a dip in a bath of fabric dye. Experiment with different strip widths for yarn of different thicknesses.

cut off bleach bottles to store string

clothes hanger wire

free newsprint (see page 19)

yarn or string inside

oatmeal box

Glass jars hold buttons, beads, colorful bits.

salt box

paint

tear off used pages

Old phone books make good surfaces for gluing.

Cottage cheese and yogurt containers – scour clean and draw or print new labels.

Reams of paper come packed in sturdy boxes perfect for files or storage.

Cardboard drums from industrial trash are good for storage or stools.

pillowcase rag bag

handy plastic buckets salvaged from restaurants

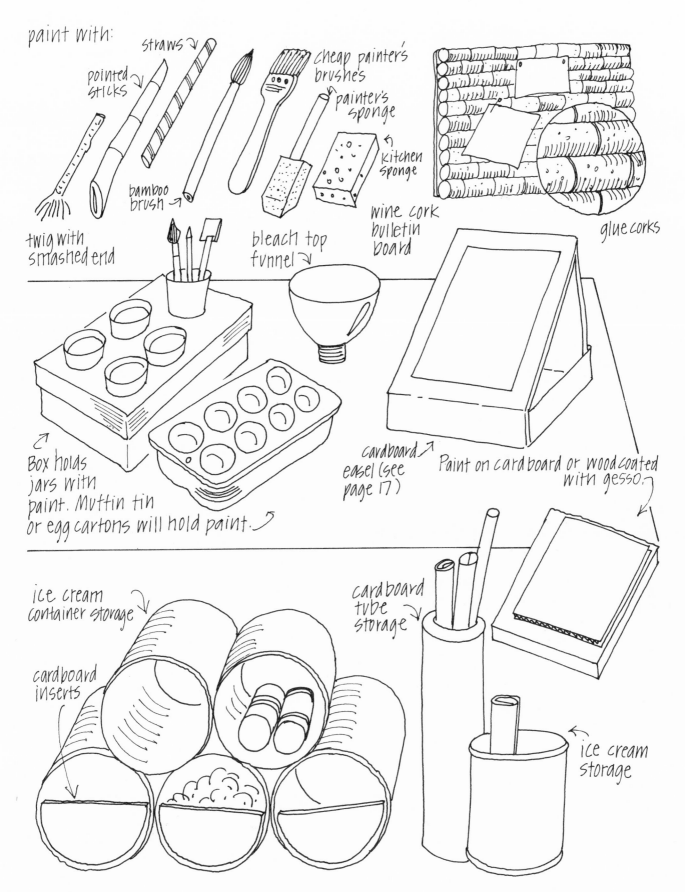

paint with:

pointed sticks

straws

cheap painters brushes

painters sponge

kitchen sponge

bamboo brush

twig with smashed end

wine cork bulletin board

glue corks

bleach top funnel

Box holds jars with paint. Muffin tin or egg cartons will hold paint.

cardboard easel (see page 17)

Paint on cardboard or wood coated with gesso.

ice cream container storage

cardboard tube storage

cardboard inserts

ice cream storage

23

Paper

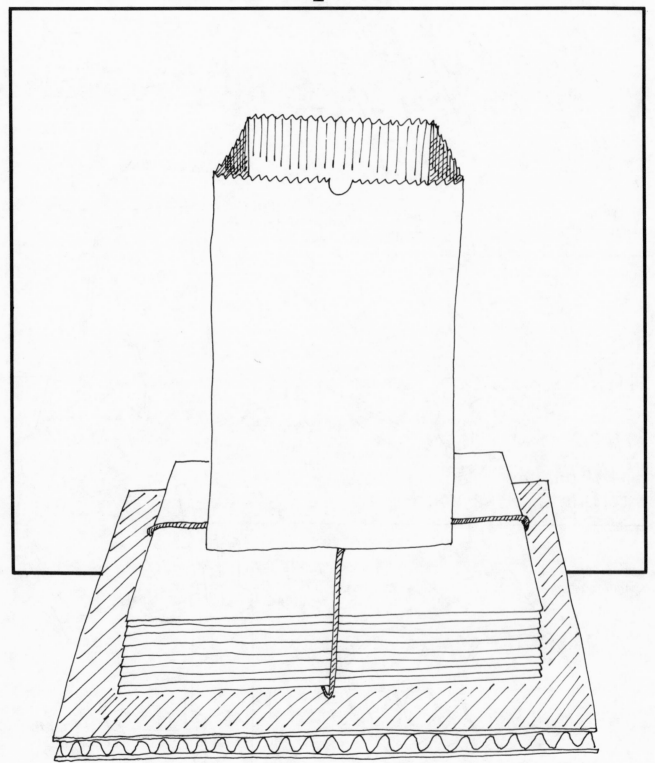

Magazine Robots

Old magazines are a handy spare parts warehouse for building a robot, a Cylon, or some other fantastic mechanical contraption. They can supply all the parts kids need for a really out-of-this-world invention. This project is an excellent one for kids who are shy about drawing. The method is called *collage* and it has been a favorite of some very famous artists.

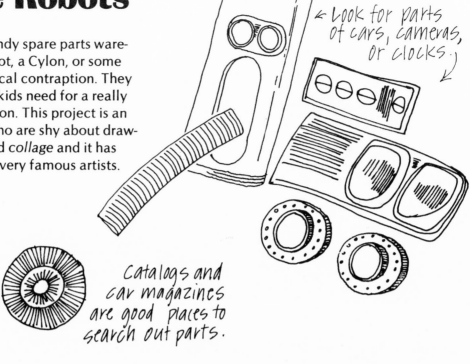

← Look for parts of cars, cameras, or clocks.

MATERIALS

Assorted magazines
Rubber cement
Sheets of paper

Catalogs and car magazines are good places to search out parts.

TOOLS

Scissors

HERE'S HOW

1. Make a robot parts stockpile. Flip through the magazines and cut out any item that might help make a robot. Look for things like stereo controls, car parts, television screens, car grills and bumpers, and kitchen equipment.
2. When you think you have a good supply of parts, assemble them into a robot. Try putting the parts together in different ways.
3. When you have a robot you like, glue it to a sheet of paper.

assembled catalog Cylon →

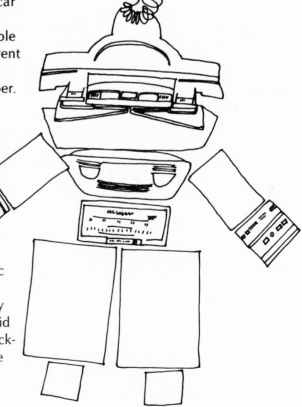

Notes: The same magazines may supply parts for prehistoric monsters, funny faces, or starships too.

There are a lot of ways to make a collage. Kids might play the "You Wanna Make Something Out of It?" game. Each kid gets a partner and gives the partner five pieces from the stockpile. The object of the game is to make something out of the parts.

Wacko Paper Hats

A few sheets of newspaper, tape, and a minute is all it takes to make an outrageous hat that looks like a cross between a cabbage and a lamp shade. With the brim rolled up, it becomes quite a respectable bowler. These hats are very useful accessories to a costume. Decorate them and hold an Easter parade. Or set up a sunbonnet booth at the school carnival and make some nickel-a-head, custom-designed sun hats to keep the crowd cool.

MATERIALS

Newspaper or sheets of clean newsprint
Tape (A roll of 2-inch masking tape is good.)
Ribbons, feathers, flowers, or other decorations

TOOLS

Stapler
Scissors
A helper

HERE'S HOW

1. Open three sheets of newspaper up flat.
2. Center the newspaper on your head.
3. Conform the paper to your head by pressing it down all around and gathering it in at about eye level. Hold the paper in position with your hands and yell for your helper.
4. Have your helper secure the paper into position with a band of tape that circles your head. It should feel snug.
5. Turn up the brim.
6. Decide how you want to finish the hat. You might just trim the brim with scissors. Or roll the edge and staple it into position. Or roll the brim all the way to the crown for the bowler model.
7. Add some ribbons, feathers, or flowers if you feel like it.

Notes: A more colorful version of this hat can be made from wallpaper samples. Stick two contrasting sheets together back-to-back with wheat paste. Or use self-sticking wallpaper that just needs water. Make the hat in the same way.

open paper

center on head

turn up brim

trim

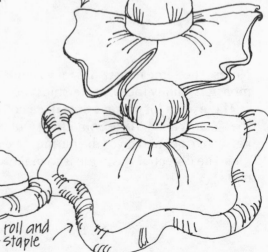

roll and staple

Boomerangs

Here is a junk version of the famous Australian aborigine's hunting weapon, the boomerang. Kids won't be able to hunt down kangaroo with it—it is strictly a toy. Boomerangs are quick to make, and kids of all ages like to launch them and watch them fly.

MATERIALS

Sheet of paper
Sheet of cardboard (The back of a writing tablet is fine for a small version. Heavy, corrugated cardboard is better for larger boomerangs.)
Paint
Clear finish (like shellac or acrylic sealant)

TOOLS

Scissors or mat knife
Paintbrush

HERE'S HOW

1. Draw and cut out a pattern for a boomerang.
2. Trace it onto a sheet of cardboard.
3. Cut it out.
4. Decorate the boomerang with painted designs. Let it dry.
5. Coat the top and bottom surface with a coat of clear finish for a shinier, longer-lasting boomerang.

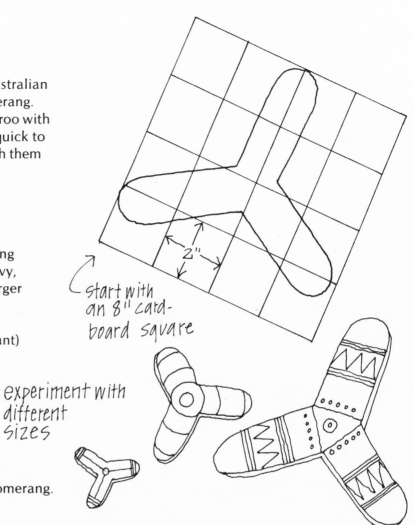

start with an 8" card- board square

2"

experiment with different sizes

Notes: To launch the boomerang put it on a flat surface, such as a book. Let one tip stick over the edge. Hit the tip with your finger or a stick in a sidewise motion. The boomerang will fly off, circle around, and land at your feet.

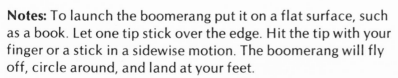

Comic Book Character and Super Hero Pins

As a matter of fact, these colorful pins don't have to be cut from comic books at all. Any interesting piece of artwork or picture from a magazine can be turned into a pin. The process is simple enough so that any kid can clip out and glue a favorite comic book character, superhero, or pet picture to pin anywhere or to give away.

MATERIALS

Magazines or comic books
Thin cardboard
White glue
Pin backs (Purchase these at a hobby store.)

TOOLS

Scissors
Paintbrushes

HERE'S HOW

1. Carefully cut out the picture you want to turn into a pin. It should be smaller than 2 inches square.
2. Cut the cardboard to the shape and size of the picture. Either measure the picture or trace the edges onto the cardboard before you cut.
3. Paint the back of the picture with white glue. Press it onto the cardboard.
4. Smooth out all the wrinkles. Put a coat of white glue over the surface of the picture. Don't worry; it will dry clear.
5. Glue the pin onto the back side.
6. For a really nice finish, give the whole thing another coat of glue—front and back, and along the edges.

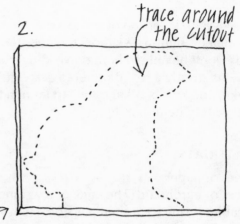

2. trace around the cutout

Cardboard backs from writing tablets are a good weight.

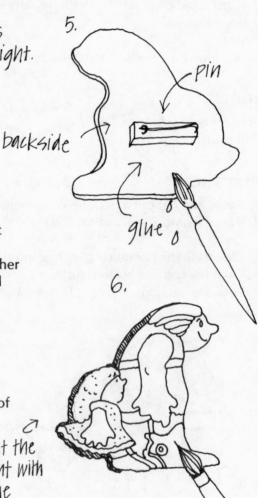

5. pin

backside

glue

6. Coat the front with glue

Buried Pictures

A nice-looking box for treasures can be made using white glue. Decorate a surface with any little bit of art, sink it under a couple of layers of this glue, which dries clear, hard, and shiny, and the result is a slick surface that looks too good to be true.

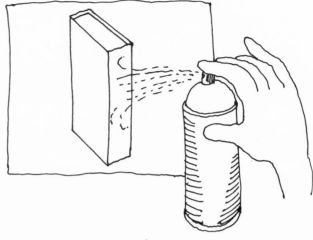

MATERIALS

Newspaper
Small box (A match box or a metal Band-Aid box will do fine.)
Can of black spray enamel
Magazines or other printed sources of pictures
White glue
Water

magazine cutout

TOOLS

Scissors
Paintbrush
Cup

HERE'S HOW

1. Cover your work area with newspaper. Paint the box with a coat of black enamel. Make sure to cover all the writing and leave a nice, even finish. Let it dry.
2. Find a picture to cut out to decorate the top of the box. The art should fit comfortably on the top, with a little space around the edges.
3. Glue the art in position on the box top.
4. Paint over the art with a layer of white glue. If the glue is thick, pour some in a cup and add water until it is the consistency of cream.
5. When it is dry, give the surface another coat of glue. Let it dry.
6. If the edges of your cutout are sunk in the surface of the glue so that they don't stick up, you are finished. If the edges do stick up, add another layer of glue.

Notes: This project is best done in warm weather. Don't hurry the drying process. Each layer needs to be really dry before the next one is added. Allow a couple of days to bury the pictures properly.

Greeting cards, seed catalogs, postcards and magazines all are good sources of cutouts.

Or try colored paper cut in a design. Or use a drawing of your own.

Magic Transfer Juice

Snoopy or Spiderman can jump from the Sunday comics and reappear on a clean sheet of paper! It's possible to create wonderful stationery, make personalized cards, or put favorite comic characters together in a special made-up picture or an altogether new comic strip. All of these things and more can happen with a little jar of Magic Transfer Juice, a mixture of turpentine, water, and soap.

MATERIALS

Turpentine
Water
Tiny piece of soap
Recent newspapers or magazines
Sheets of paper

TOOLS

Small glass jar with a tight-fitting lid
Paintbrush
Spoon
Scissors

HERE'S HOW

1. First you need to mix some Magic Transfer Juice. Start by pouring a little turpentine into the glass jar.
2. Pour in about four times as much water. Lines drawn on the side of the jar might make this job easier.
3. Add a tiny piece of soap to help mix the turpentine with the water. Put on the lid and shake up the juice. Your Magic Transfer Juice is ready to use.
4. Cut out a picture you want to transfer. Use a fresh newspaper for starters.
5. Paint the back of the picture with the Magic Transfer Juice.
6. Let the fluid soak through the picture for a minute.

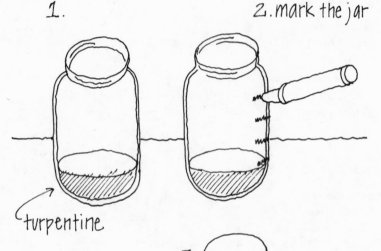

1.

2. mark the jar

turpentine

3.

soap

water

shake

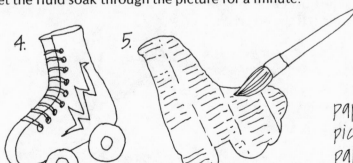

4.

5.

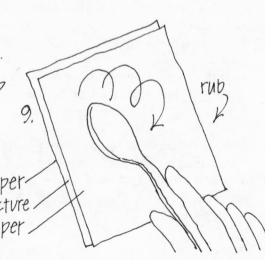

9.

paper
picture
paper

rub

7. Put the picture face down on the sheet of paper that you want to transfer it onto. Be careful when you do this so that you don't smear it.
8. Cover the transfer picture with a clean sheet of paper.
9. Rub over the surface of the picture with the back of a spoon. Be careful not to tear the paper. Do a good job of rubbing every part.
10. Remove the sheet of paper and peel away the newspaper or magazine picture. Let it dry for a minute. The new picture may look a little odd because it's backwards.

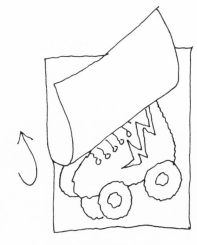

10. peel away

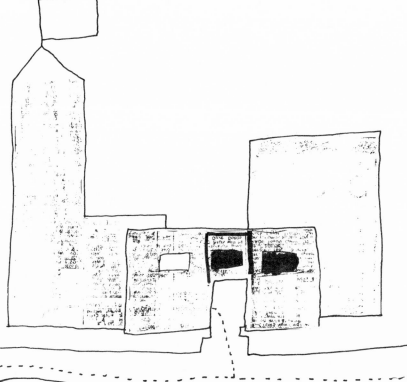

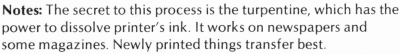

Notes: The secret to this process is the turpentine, which has the power to dissolve printer's ink. It works on newspapers and some magazines. Newly printed things transfer best.

Transfer pictures onto any kind of paper to make special cards and drawings. Try cutting out hearts for a valentine card. Or cut shapes of skyscrapers out of the want ads, rub them onto paper, and draw over them for a city scene. Or cut some lacy snowflakes out of a magazine page and transfer them onto stiff paper for a Christmas card.

Fold-Up Boxes

Here's a neat little gift box that needs no glue, no tape, and no staples. Is it done with mirrors? No. The secret is in the folding. All that's needed is a pair of heavyweight magazine pages. The more colorful the pages, the prettier the box. A page that measures 8½ by 11 inches will make a box about 4 by 5 inches.

MATERIALS

Magazine pages

HERE'S HOW

1. Crease the magazine page to mark the center line from left to right and from top to bottom. Open it flat.
2. Fold the top and bottom ends to the center crease.
3. Fold the sides to the center. Open them up.
4. Fold all four corners to the creases that you just made in step 3.
5. Fold back the edges that run down the center over the corner triangles.
6. Pull the borders apart to form the box.
7. Pinch the corners and crease around the edges to give the box shape.
8. Fold up another box the same size for the lid.

Notes: These boxes are nice for holding lightweight gifts. Since the walls are only a single sheet, they are easy to squash. Try folding up two sheets at once for a box with extra strength.

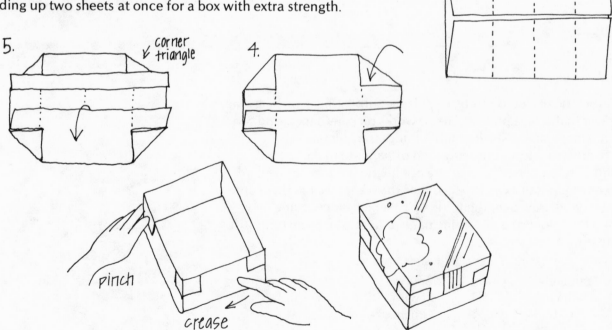

 32

Fish Kites

These flying fish are not ordinary, high-in-the-sky flying kites. However, they do have big, round mouths and hollow bodies for catching the wind. Staked outside on a pole, they twist and turn and seem to swim in the air. Carp kites are a special decoration made to celebrate the Boys' Festival on Children's Day in Japan, which is on May 5. But any time of year these flying fish are fun to make and will look splendid decorating a ceiling or adding some flying colors to the next outdoor celebration.

MATERIALS

Large sheet of paper (Newsprint rolls are perfect.)
Glue
Plastic top (Any circular top, like the lid to an ice cream container, measuring at least 5 inches will do.)
Paint or markers (See **Roll-On Markers,** page 20.)
String

TOOLS

Scissors
Yardstick
Paintbrush
Stapler

HERE'S HOW

1. Cut a piece of paper 20 inches by 30 inches.
2. Fold it in half lengthwise.
3. Draw on the outline of a fish using the illustration as a guide.
4. Cut it out.
5. Glue or staple the long edge closed.
6. Paint or draw on fish scales, fins, and eyes.
7. Cut out the center of the plastic top to make a ring.
8. Insert the ring into the carp's mouth. Fold the paper over it and staple it into position.
9. Add the strings.
10. Tie it up. It's best in a breeze.

Notes: Instead of paper, old sheets can be turned into a sturdier cloth fish kite. Decorate the fish with fabric crayons or felt markers. Stitch the body shut. Finish it in the same way.

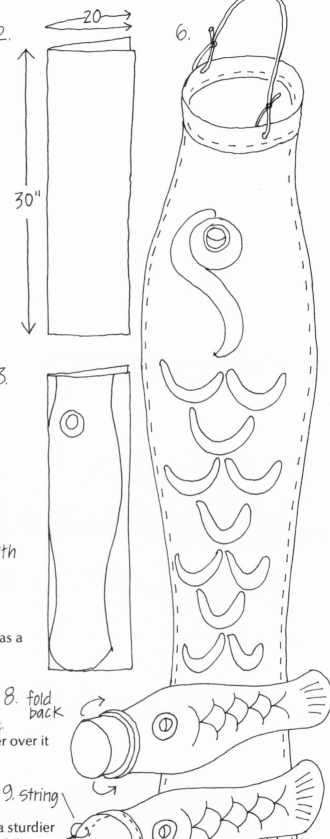

2.

30"

20

3.

6.

7. plastic top from coffee can

cut out center

ring for mouth

8. fold back

9. string

33

Stained Glass Windows

A wax paper-and-crayon stained glass window looks wonderful with the light coming through it, making all its colors glow. This art project is good for decorating a window that somebody is tired of looking out of, or one that somebody doesn't want other people looking into. One of the best things about making crayon stained glass is that it uses up old stumps of crayons that are impossible to draw with anyway.

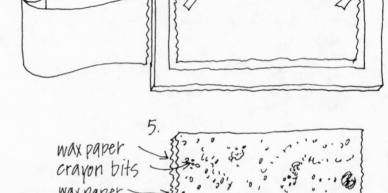

MATERIALS

Assorted crayons in bright colors
Wax paper
Newspaper
Tape

TOOLS

Grater (The four-sided, upright kind that you find in the kitchen is best.)
Cups
Scissors
Iron (and a surface to iron on)

HERE'S HOW

1. Shred the crayons by rubbing them on the grater. Be careful not to shred your fingers!
2. Collect the crayon gratings into cups. Use a different cup for each color.
3. Measure the wax paper to fit the window you want to turn into a stained glass window. Cut the wax paper to size.
4. Cut another piece of wax paper the same size.
5. Sprinkle the crayon bits onto the sheet of wax paper. You can arrange them carefully in a design or just scatter the colors onto the sheet. Make sure to get some crayon bits on all parts of the paper.

newspaper
crayon sandwich

6. When you have the crayon bits spread out, lay the other sheet of wax paper on the top.
7. Set the wax paper sandwich between some sheets of newspaper.
8. Press the newspaper with a warm iron. The iron should be just warm enough to melt the wax. Iron all the parts to get a good melted sandwich.
9. Take away the newspaper and see what happened.
10. Tape the stained glass to the window so that the light shines through the melted crayon.
11. For a fancier window, accordion fold the melted sandwich. Cut out some triangles with a pair of scissors. This will make a lacy diamond design.

11.

 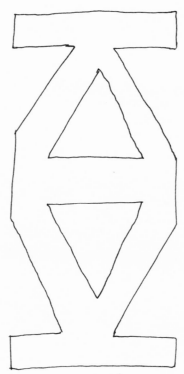 

Notes: Make sure to put down paper on the table or work area first. All those little bits of crayons can make a mess.

Stained glass windows look best if they are made with light, bright crayon colors like orange, red, yellow, and pink. Use dark colors sparingly. If the stained glass window has valleys of no color, try pressing it again with the warm iron. If that doesn't fix it, make another using a bit more crayon. But don't get too heavy-handed with the crayons, or the stained glass window will turn into muck.

Give the design some structure by mounting the melt in a frame of black construction paper. Glue on divider strips to resemble the leading in stained glass.

Books for Long Stories

The models for these accordion-fold books are books from Japan which often contain haiku poems. Kids can use them for scrapbooks, journals, or for a very long story. Blank books with good-looking covers make top notch presents.

Accordion-fold books require a source of long paper. Trimmings from the big sheets that printers use are perfect. Better than perfect would be a sheet of billboard paper that is printed with intriguing designs on one side and is blank on the other. The books can be made to any dimensions. These instructions are for paper that is 22 inches long, a standard size.

MATERIALS

Paper (at least 22 inches long)
Cardboard
Decorative paper or fabric for the covers
Rubber cement
Ribbon

TOOLS

Scissors
Ruler
Mat knife or paper cutter
Glue

HERE'S HOW

1. Cut a strip of paper for the pages. It should be 3½ inches wide and at least 22 inches long.
2. Accordion fold the strip every 3½ inches. Trim off any excess. A mat knife or paper cutter is best for this job.
3. Cut two 4-inch cardboard squares for the covers.
4. Cut two 5-inch squares of a print fabric or pretty paper for the covers.
5. Spread the cardboard squares with rubber cement and press on the covering material. Take care to smooth out the wrinkles. Make sure to leave a ½-inch margin all around.
6. Fold the side margins around to the back. Glue them down.
7. Fold the end flaps around to the back. Glue them down. For a neater job, make angled corners as shown.

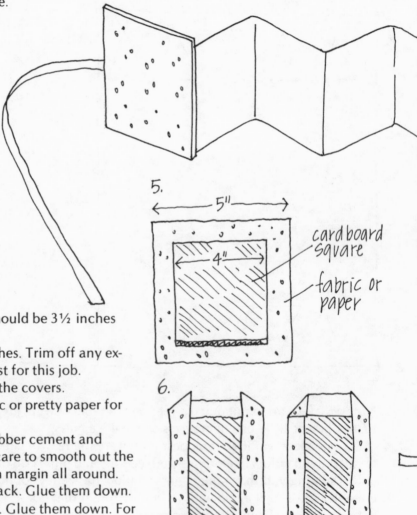

5.

5"

4"

cardboard square

fabric or paper

6.

8. Glue the cover to the end pages. First spread one end of the accordion fold strip with rubber cement. Press it onto the cover, making sure it is centered. Do the same at the other end to make the back cover.
9. Accordion fold the book shut.
10. Glue in a pair of ribbons as a closing device for a very personal book.

Notes: There are all sorts of junk possibilities for attractive cover materials. Use a scrap of fabric, magazine pages, a road map or some old giftwrap. Or use a drawing, marbled paper, or a print from one of the projects in this book. Experiment making some long horizontal books and some tall skinny ones.

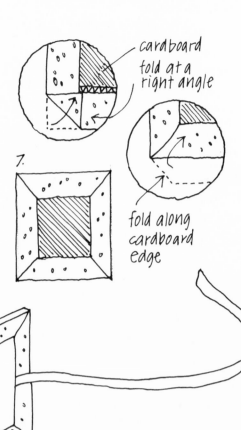

cardboard
fold at a
right angle

fold along
cardboard
edge

7.

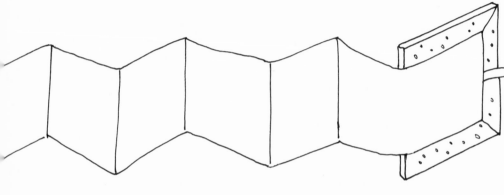

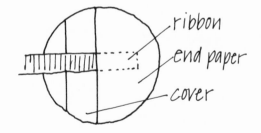

ribbon

end paper

cover

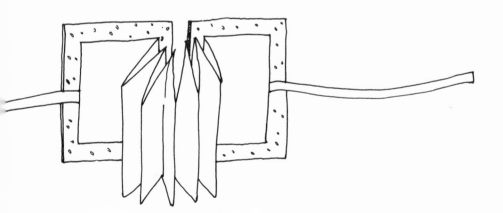

Ribands

Ribands are paper decorations that are made in Poland for festive occasions. They are, perhaps, the source of our own rosettes and blue ribbon awards. Kids can make ribands for a school awards ceremony, for the Best Mom Ever or Best Dad Ever (or Most Dapper Dog), or for contest prizes.

MATERIALS

Assorted paper (Collect any lightweight paper, such as gift wrap, tissue, or bits of metallic paper from the inside of candy wrappers.)
Foil stars (from the stationery store)
Glue

TOOLS

Scissors
Ruler
Pen or colored marker

streamers:

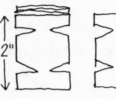 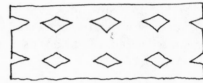

tips:

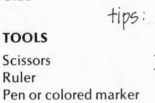 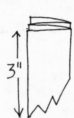 one tip

one tip

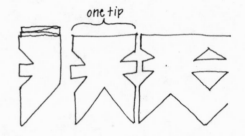

HERE'S HOW TO MAKE THE STREAMERS

1. Cut two strips of paper 2 inches wide and about 8 inches long.
2. To make fancy streamers, accordion fold the strips and cut some designs into the edges.

HERE'S HOW TO MAKE THE TIPS

1. Cut a strip of paper about 3 inches wide and about 8 inches long.
2. Accordion fold it every 2 inches.
3. Cut it along one edge in a way similar to the illustration.
4. Cut off a pair of 2-inch sections. These will be your tips.

HERE'S HOW TO MAKE THE MEDALLION

1. Cut a 5-inch square of paper.
2. Fold it in half diagonally.
3. Fold it in half again diagonally. Open it up.
4. Fold points A and B to point C.
5. Fold points D and E to the center fold.
6. Fold the whole job in half.
7. Clip off the tip.
8. Cut a design into the folded medallion.
9. Open it up and press it flat.

medallions:

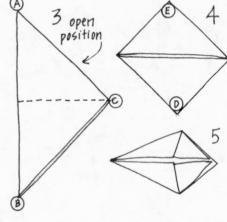

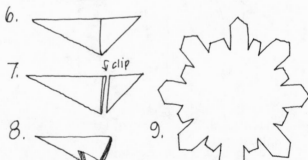

HERE'S HOW TO ASSEMBLE THE RIBAND

1. Glue the fancy tips to the streamers.
2. Glue the medallions one on top of the other if you are using more than one layer.
3. Glue the streamers to the underside of the medallion.
4. Add foil stars for some extra sparkle.
5. If the riband is to be awarded for a special occasion, you might want to inscribe it with some appropriate words and the date.

medallion, variations:

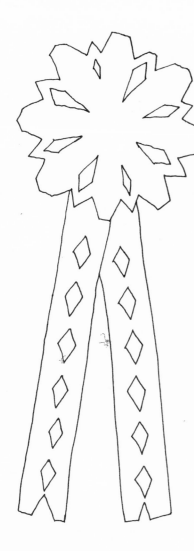

Notes: All sorts of materials can be cut into ribands. Junk mail, scraps of gift wrap, the tissue that comes wrapped around shoes, and brown paper bags will all work. Add some glitter with bits of foil from candy wrappers. Try dipping the edges of streamers and tips in cups of food coloring that has been thinned with water for some extra colorful effects. This works especially well on tissue paper. Let it dry before assembling it.

For a multi-layered medallion cut three from different size squares.

Strip Papier-Mâché

Papier mâché is a classic trash artist's recipe. With the help of some sticky stuff like starch or wheat paste, kids can turn old paper into almost any shape and it will dry rock hard. Artists in the eighteenth century used it to make fine furniture for the French kings. Kids today can mold it into wild animals five feet tall, sculpt puppets with funny faces, or build miniature boxes. Papier mâché can do almost anything.

There are two basic ways to make papier mâché. One is to make a modeling dough which can be treated like clay. The other is strip papier mâché, a method more suited to large-scale projects.

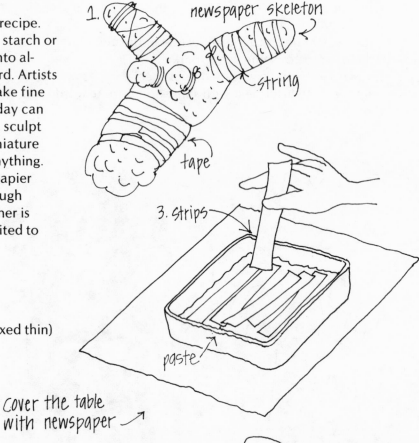

1. newspaper skeleton
string
tape

3. Strips
paste

Cover the table with newspaper →

MATERIALS

Newspaper
Liquid starch or wheatpaper paste (mixed thin)
Sandpaper
Tempera paint
Shellac or acrylic sealant

TOOLS

Bowl
Paintbrush

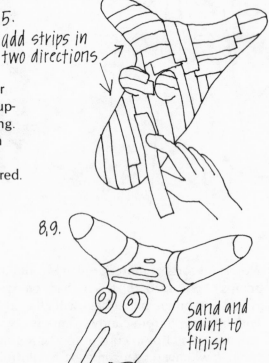

5. add strips in two directions

8,9.
Sand and paint to finish

HERE'S HOW

1. For this method you need a skeleton which you will cover with papier mâché. For instance if you want to make a puppet head, wad up some newspaper and bind it with a string. For large animals like a 4-foot kangaroo, build a skeleton out of wood and chicken wire. Don't worry about how it looks. It just has to hold together long enough to get covered.
2. Tear the newspaper into strips.
3. Drag the strips through the starch or paste to coat them.
4. Lay them over the skeleton so they go in one direction. Cover the whole surface.
5. Put on another layer in the opposite direction.
6. Do this three or four times
7. Let the mâché dry. It will take a couple of days.
8. Sand the mâché for a smooth surface.
9. Paint it with tempera.
10. Coat it with shellac or acrylic sealant to give it a waterproof, shiny surface.

Papier-Mâché Clay

Papier mâché clay is a modeling compound similar to regular modeling clay. Shape it into just about anything—a dish, a head, buttons, or jewelry. Here's a no-cook recipe that's easy to make.

MATERIALS

Water
Newspaper
Wheat paste (from a hobby store or wallpaper
    supply)
Sandpaper
Tempera paint
Shellac or acrylic sealant

TOOLS

Bucket
Spoon or electric beater
Paintbrush

HERE'S HOW

1. Fill the bucket halfway with water.
2. Tear the newspaper into 1-inch squares.
3. Add them to the water. Let them soak overnight.
4. Beat the paper bits to a pulp. An electric beater will hurry the process.
5. Squeeze out the water so the mass is damp.
6. Add the wheat paste a bit at a time as you beat the pulp. Keep beating until you have a smooth, claylike mass.
7. Mold the mâché clay into something.
8. Let it dry. This will take three to five days, depending on the size of the object.
9. Sand and paint your mâché clay sculpture.
10. Give it a coat of sealant.

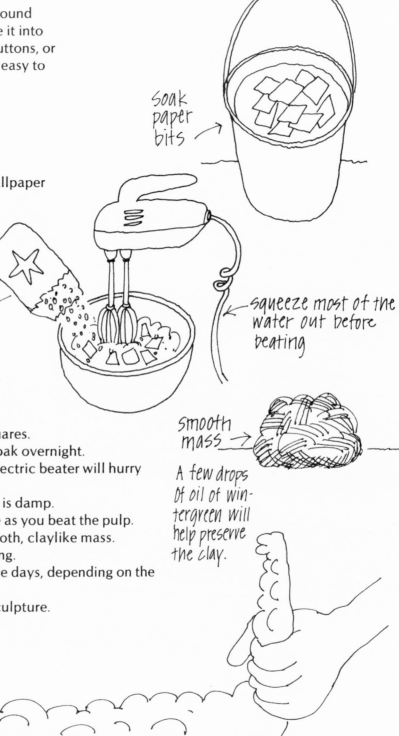

soak paper bits

wheat paste

squeeze most of the water out before beating

smooth mass →

A few drops of oil of wintergreen will help preserve the clay.

Marbelous Gift Bags

"Ooh! Look at this one!" "Oh wow! Look at that one!" "Let me do just one more!"

That's the kind of conversation overheard around a pan where marbled paper is being made. Some of the kids who made marbled paper said it was the best art project they ever did. One thing is sure—it's a good way to turn an ordinary paper bag into a gift wrap that will knock your socks off.

MATERIALS

Newspaper
Water
Oil-based paint (Old tubes of artist's oils, jars of model paint, and leftover cans of enamel wall paint will all work.)
Turpentine or paint thinner
Small paper bags (White ones are especially nice.)

TOOLS

Apron (See **Newspaper Aprons,** page 18.)
Pan or tray (larger than the paper bags)
Stick
Tongs or gloves

HERE'S HOW

1. Spread some newspaper on the surface you want to work on. Put on an apron. This can be a messy project.
2. Fill the pan with ½-inch of water.
3. Pour some of the paint into the water. If the colors are thick and sticky, thin them with turpentine or paint thinner first.
4. Drop in some other colors.
5. Swirl the paint around with a stick to make an interesting pattern.
6. Lay the paper bag down on the liquid surface. Tap the bag a few times to make sure it picks up the paint.
7. Using tongs or wearing gloves, lift up one corner of the paper and pull it away.
8. Repeat the process for the other side.
9. Set the marbled paper bags out to dry. This can take up to a day if the puddles of paint are thick.

(coat the pan with salad oil for easy clean up)

5.

stick or soda straw

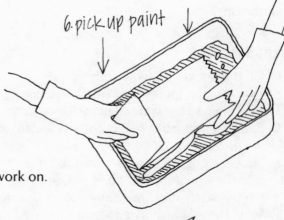

6. pick up paint

7. drain

Notes: With a little practice it is possible to control the design and make waves and swirls, or big puddles and pools — perhaps even draw something with the rivers of color. Gold looks especially nice. Buy a little bottle of gold paint at a hobby store that sells models. In fact, a hobby store is a good place to buy small amounts of any colors for experimenting.

The marble method works just fine on sheets of paper that can be used for letter writing, book covers, or flat gift wrap. Try marbling a pencil or a piece of fabric. Use the thinner to clean up afterwards.

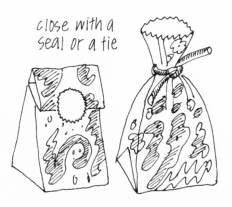

close with a seal or a tie

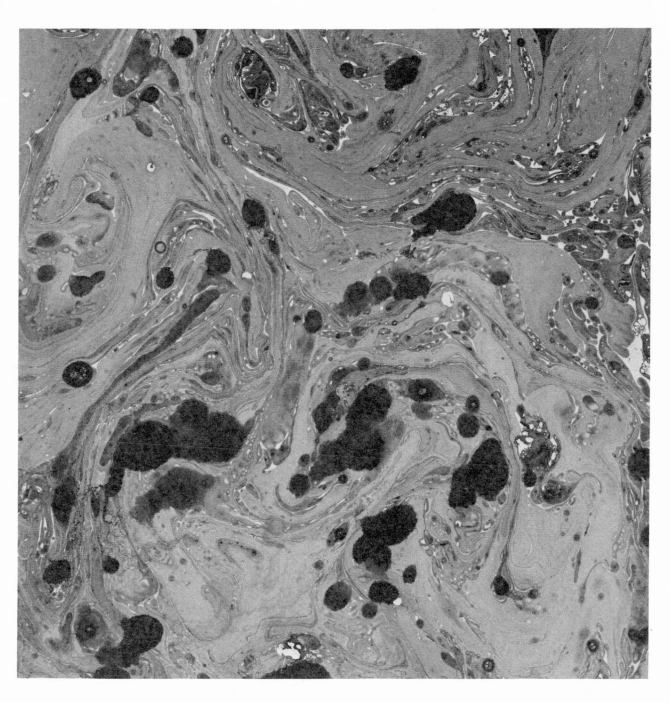

Paper Garland

Paper garlands are an easy decoration to make using only a bit of paper and a few quick snips with the scissors. Pin them up by one end, and let them blow and turn in the wind. Or join several together for a long chain. Use newsprint, magazine pages or even old envelopes.

MATERIALS

Paper (Any kind will do, but stiff paper is best.)

TOOLS

Scissors
Staples or tape

HERE'S HOW

1. Cut a piece of paper into a rectangle. Fold it in half lengthwise.
2. Make 10 cuts across but not all the way through to the other edge. Stop 1 inch away from the opposite side. Space your cuts evenly.
3. Turn the rectangle around. Make 11 cuts in the same way, dividing the segments made by the cuts in step 2 in half.
4. Pull the ends in opposite directions to open up the garland.
5. For a single garland that is twice as long, cut along the fold as shown. Clip one end.
6. Cut several and tape or staple the ends together for extra long garlands.

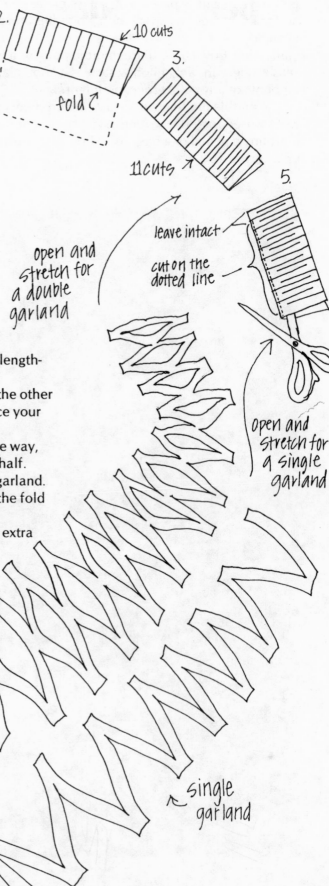

2. ← 10 cuts
fold

3. 11 cuts

open and stretch for a double garland

5. leave intact
cut on the dotted line

open and stretch for a single garland

double garland

single garland

44

Paper Pagodas

These old-time tricks of paper cutting are an easy way to turn a sheet of paper into a whole set of complicated-looking loops. Cut up a whole bunch from junk paper—of course the more colorful the better—and pin them up for party decorations.

MATERIALS

Paper
String

TOOLS

Scissors
Stapler

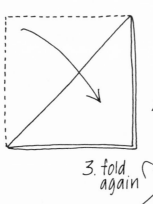

2. fold in half

3. fold again 4. make cuts

HERE'S HOW TO MAKE A PAGODA

1. Cut a piece of paper into a square.
2. Fold the paper in half diagonally.
3. Fold it in half again.
4. Make three cuts as shown in the drawing.
5. Open it up.
6. Knot a string in the center of the middle square.
7. Hang it up.

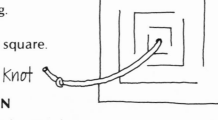

6.

Knot

string

7.

HERE'S HOW TO MAKE A PAGODA CHAIN

1. Cut an even number of small paper pagodas. Twelve pagodas cut from 4-inch squares will make a nice chain.
2. Staple them together in pairs at the corners. Do this for the whole lot.
3. Shake them to open the pagoda pairs.
4. Connect the pagoda pairs by joining the squares at the top and bottom with a stapler. Do this so that you have a whole string of them.
5. Hang the chain for some cheap frills.

Note: Experiment with more cuts on each pagoda for lighter versions.

2. staple corners

3. shake apart

4. join to make chain

Plastic

Amazing Shrinking Tops

The process of shrinking these tops is almost like magic. Draw on them, bake them, and watch them shrink into teeny circles. The drawing shrinks in the bargain. The secret is in the plastic. Use only the clear, lightweight circles that cover pint-sized containers of meat (like liver). One clue is that they sometimes have a red rim. These amazing tops make an unusual key chain or I.D. tag.

MATERIALS

Plastic lids
Felt markers

TOOLS

Paper punch
Scissors
Metal cookie sheet
Oven or toaster oven
Pot holder
Pancake turner

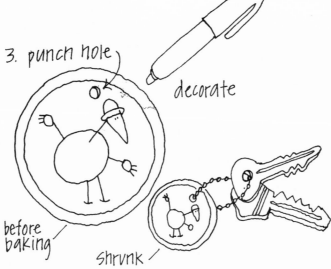

3. punch hole
decorate
before baking
shrunk

HERE'S HOW

1. First the lid needs to be cleaned. Soak the paper label off in warm water. Scrape the lid clean.
2. Decorate the lid with felt marker designs. Experiment to find the pens that draw on plastic with the brightest colors. You can erase any mistakes in drawing with a wet finger.
3. If you want to be able to attach the lid to something, you need to punch a hole in the disk *before* it bakes.
4. Put the lid on a metal cookie sheet. Set the oven at 400°F. Bake the lid for about two minutes until it is flat.
5. If your lid comes out crinkly, press it flat with a pancake turner while it is warm.

Note: It is also possible to cut out a shape from a liver lid, then decorate and shrink it in the same way.

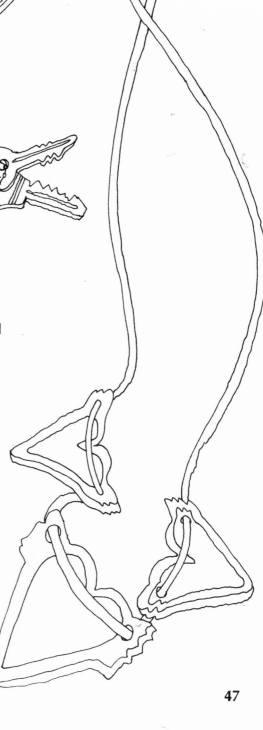

shapes can be worn as jewels →

WALTER FLAX'S FLEET

Walter Flax has a whole fleet of battle ships in his backyard in Yorktown, Virginia. There are hundreds of them and they all float, even though none of them has ever sailed on a sea. Walter has tested each one in a tub for sea-worthiness.

There are ships of all sorts—battleships, cruisers, and gunships. He built each one of these beauties from found materials. They look real enough until you get up close and see that they are made from pieces of phones, clocks, bike parts, lamps, cans, ashtrays, plumbers' hardware, and wire.

Walter has observed real ships but says these days he gets most of his ideas from magazines. The ships measure from 2 feet to 25 feet and would make an impressive sight if ever he got his whole fleet into a body of water. Walter hopes to do just that someday.

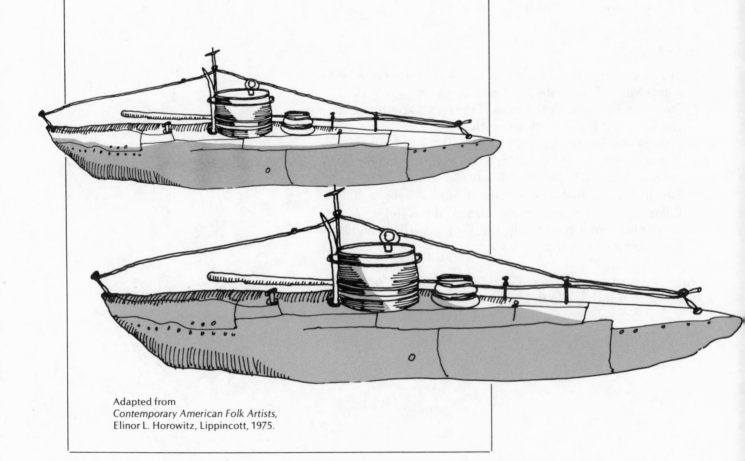

Adapted from
Contemporary American Folk Artists,
Elinor L. Horowitz, Lippincott, 1975.

Foam Boats

A chunk of Styrofoam is the basic ingredient for a whole navy of unsinkable ships. Ask at appliance or department stores for the odd pieces of foam that come packed around appliances and televisions. All that's needed to complete the fleet is a handful of odds and ends. Then find a place to launch it.

hulls can be any shape

MATERIALS

Styrofoam pieces (Flat pieces are best, but corners will work.)
Odds and ends (lightweight things like berry baskets, pins, nails, small blocks of wood, tubes, string, twigs)
White glue

twig → _cloth_

tape

TOOLS

Scissors
Serrated knife or small saw

glued spools for stacks

corner piece of foam packing

HERE'S HOW

1. Cut the hull from the foam. Use scissors for thin Styrofoam and a serrated knife for the thicker kind.
2. Stick on a cabin, smokestacks, sails, a rail all around the deck, and portholes. Use whatever you have, letting the individual shapes of the odds and ends suggest how they will be used.
3. Stick them into the foam. You might have to add a drop of glue to make them secure.
4. Find a body of water and see if she floats. Then build up an entire navy.

bottle corks

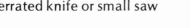

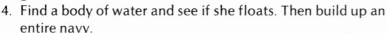

cork

plastic cup   _cap_

wood block

cardboard box

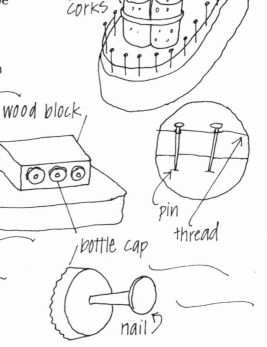

bottle cap

pin
thread

nail

Styrofoam Stamps

Styrofoam cups, the kind that collect in great piles around the coffee machines or in fast food restaurants, are the basic materials for these big stamps that can be used to print with again and again. Styrofoam stamps can be used to decorate stationery or envelopes, and to make a nice gift card. Or they can be used to print up some fancy wrapping paper.

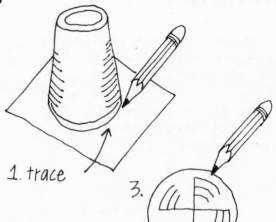

1. trace

3.

MATERIALS

Styrofoam cups and lids
Styrofoam trays (the kind that you get from the meat market)
White glue
Stamp pad or poster paint
Paper

5.
lid →
drawing →

6. paint →

TOOLS

Ball-point pen or a pencil
Scissors

7.
stamp

HERE'S HOW

1. Turn the cup upside down on the foam tray. Trace around the mouth so that you leave a mark on the tray.
2. Cut out the shape.
3. Draw a design on the shape with the pen or pencil. Remember that these lines will print white on a dark background. Draw with a gentle pressure to leave a clean line in the soft Styrofoam.
4. Put the lid on the cup.
5. Glue the drawing onto the lid of the cup. Let it dry.
6. Coat the design with ink from a stamp pad or thick poster paint.
7. Press the inky design onto some paper for a print.

Notes: Cut out fancy shapes like animals, arrows, or hearts for your next Styrofoam stamp. Decorate them with drawings or print with them as plain shapes.

print with squares
cut from the styrofoam
trays

Squirt Pictures

"It's a lady on a cloud." "No, it's a ghost." "No, it's a man on a bike in space." Squirt pictures can't help but push imaginations into high gear. And it's no wonder. These paintings are big, colorful versions of the old inkblot tests that psychologists use for just that purpose. Ordinary painting materials and some squirt bottles are all that's needed. It's the squirt that makes the difference.

MATERIALS

Poster paint (Three colors are good to start with.)
Water
Sheets of paper (Newsprint is fine.)

TOOLS

Plastic squeeze bottles (The kind that hold liquid detergent are fine. You will need one for each color.)

HERE'S HOW

1. Mix the paint with water so that it pours like thick cream.
2. Pour it into the bottles.
3. Fold a sheet of paper in half. Open it up.
4. To make the painting, squirt a squiggle of paint on one side of the fold. The secret is to use a small amount of paint.
5. Fold the paper in half again and press out the puddles of paint.
6. Open it up and see what happened.
7. Repeat the process with other colors.
8. When you are finished adding colors, let the painting dry.

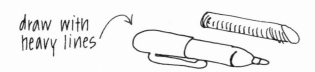

draw with heavy lines

Notes: Hang the painting just as it is and enjoy it as a design. Or look for a picture in those blots and puddles of paint. Draw over the design with a dark marker or crayon to make the picture look more like what the squirt suggests. Make up a title to write at the bottom of the picture.

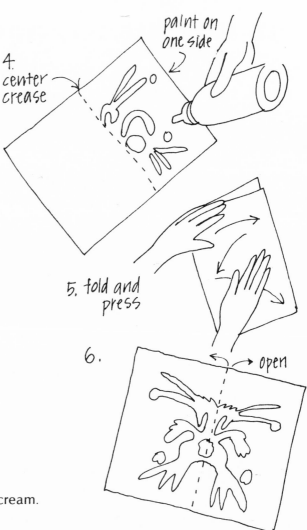

4. center crease

paint on one side

5. fold and press

6. open

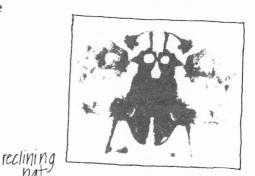

reclining bat

Russian dancer

Jug Heads

Who but a trash artist would look at a plastic jug and see mummies, barn owls, star warriors, and people from outer space? These bizarre masks are a snap to make for any kid with enough skill to cut up a plastic jug. Bleach bottles, or water or juice jugs in gallon or half-gallon sizes are the basic material. They come in a lot of different shapes, so the masks will look quite different from each other. With some careful cutting, it's possible to get two masks from each bottle.

MATERIALS

Plastic jug
Two 12-inch lengths of string
Felt markers or acrylic paint

TOOLS

Pointed scissors
A helper
Paper punch
Sandpaper
Paintbrush

HERE'S HOW

1. Trace the shape of the mask onto the bottle. Let the markings on the plastic help you decide where to cut.
2. Cut out the mask. Use scissors with a point. Strong hands may be needed to cut through the thick parts.
3. Punch holes on each side of the mask. Insert and knot the ties.
4. Try on the mask. Have your helper mark the spots for the eyeholes. Remove the mask and cut them out.
5. Sand the edges if they seem rough or ragged.
6. Decorate the mask with felt markers or acrylic paint.

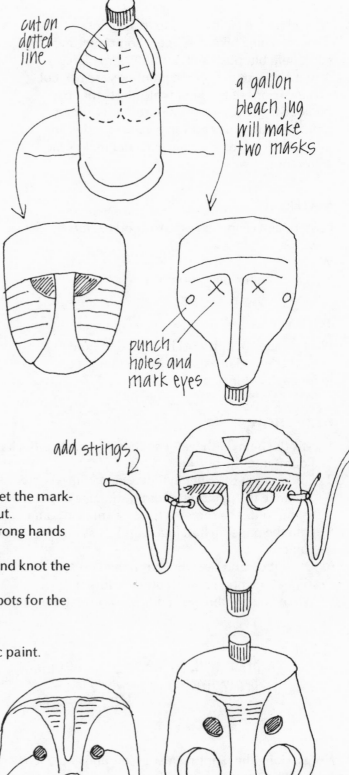

cut on dotted line

a gallon bleach jug will make two masks

punch holes and mark eyes

add strings

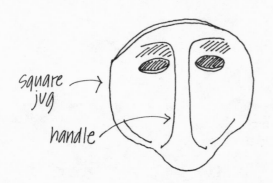

square jug

handle

water jug

52

Plastic Sandwiches

These plastic sandwiches, or laminations, make unusual cards or permanent pages for scrap-books. They are also a special way to preserve a collection of little things. Besides, they are just plain fun to make.

MATERIALS

Plastic sandwich bags (Thin ones work best.)
Something to sandwich (Use flat things, such as paper or fabric.)
Aluminum foil

TOOLS

Scissors
Iron (and a surface to iron on)

HERE'S HOW

1. Arrange the things you want to laminate between the sheets of plastic. The best results are with little items or something that has holes in it, such as lace. You might have to trim things to make them fit. The plastic needs to stick together at regular intervals.
2. Put your plastic sandwich between two sheets of aluminum foil.
3. Press it with a warm iron.
4. Peel away the foil. Trim the edges to make it look tidy. Presto! You've made a plastic sandwich.

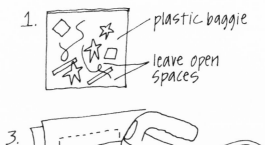

1. plastic baggie
leave open spaces

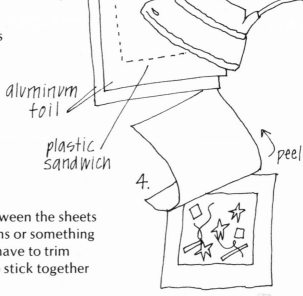

3.
aluminum foil
plastic sandwich
peel
4.

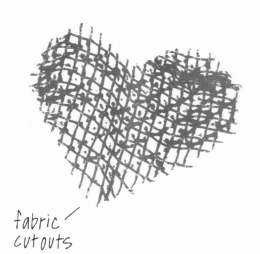

fabric cutouts

little photos

glitter, stickers, foil stars

You can also use mesh, yarn, string, or words cut from newspapers.

Plastic Letters

Every once in a while it is handy to have around big letters to print up a sign or a poster. This is a cheap and easy way to make them using nothing more than the plastic lids that cover coffee cans. Cut up a freeform set or use a pattern to cut a precision set of block letters.

MATERIALS

Plastic lids (The flexible vinyl sort that cover coffee cans are good. For a whole alphabet you'll need quite a few.)
Thick piece of cardboard (larger than letters) or a Styrofoam block
Stamp pad

TOOLS

Ball-point pen or felt marker
Pointed scissors or mat knife
Straight edge

HERE'S HOW

1. Draw or trace the letters onto the plastic lids. Clear plastic lids make tracing easier.
2. Carefully cut out the letters. Make the edges as smooth as you can.
3. Mount the letter backwards on a thick piece of cardboard or a Styrofoam block.
4. Press each letter onto the stamp pad. Print it.

Notes: Try designing a set of letters based on a half circle. The easiest letters to cut are block letters without curlicues or serifs. The local library should have a book of alphabets to use for a pattern. Or use the pattern provided here.

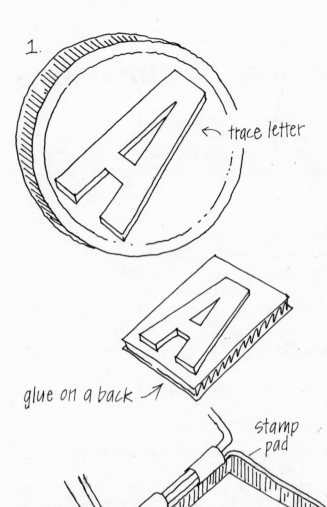

1.

← trace letter

glue on a back ↗

stamp pad

3.
press to print
↓

You can print without mounting the letters on backs, but you risk inky fingers.

ABCDEFG
HIJKLMN
OPQRSTU
VWXYZ&
12345678
90O$

glue on a handle

Soda Straw Loom

Who would have thought that four plastic soda straws side by side would make a loom? Not only do they make a loom, but they make one that is quick to construct, a cinch to use, cheap, and portable. The soda straw loom is best for weaving long, thin things like straps and belts. Try it out using fat **T-Shirt Yarn** (see page 21), or leftover scraps of yarn.

MATERIALS

4 plastic soda straws
4 beads (large enough to keep from slipping into the straws)
Yarn (Thick yarn gives the quickest results.)

TOOLS

Scissors
Yardstick

HERE'S HOW

1. To weave a belt cut four strands of yarn about 2 yards long.
2. Thread a bead onto the middle of each strand of yarn.
3. Thread a strand of yarn through each straw as shown in the illustration. Sucking on the straw will help pull the yarn through.
4. Straighten out the threads. Knot the eight loose ends together. Your loom is ready for weaving.
5. To begin weaving, hold a ball of yarn in one hand and the loom in the other. The straws must be side by side.
6. Wind the yarn from the ball over and under, over and under the straws. Loop the yarn around the end straw and weave back in an under and over fashion in the opposite direction.
7. Keep weaving, pushing your weaving downwards as you go.
8. When your weaving is long enough to fit around your waist (if you are making a belt), clip the beads off.
9. Slide off the straws.
10. Gather up the ends and make a knot.
11. Tie it on.

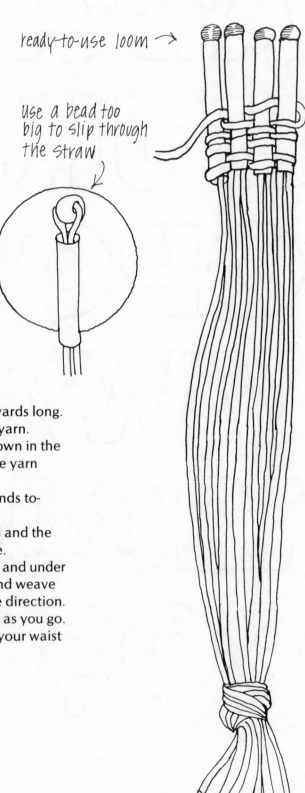

ready-to-use loom →

use a bead too big to slip through the straw

Notes: Weave with bands of different colors by changing the yarn. Just knot another color on. Use more straws for a wider weaving. The limit is as many straws as can be handled with one hand.

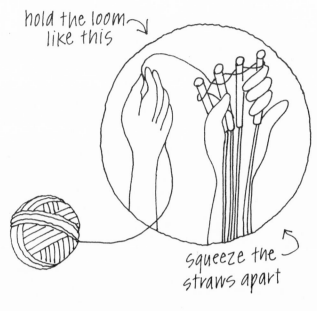

hold the loom like this

squeeze the straws apart

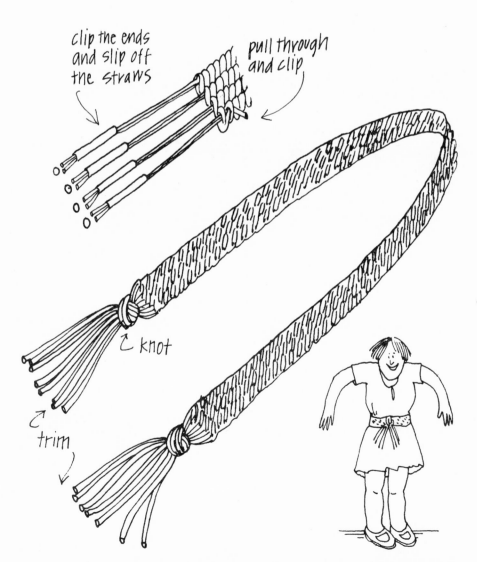

clip the ends and slip off the straws

pull through and clip

↶ knot

↶ trim

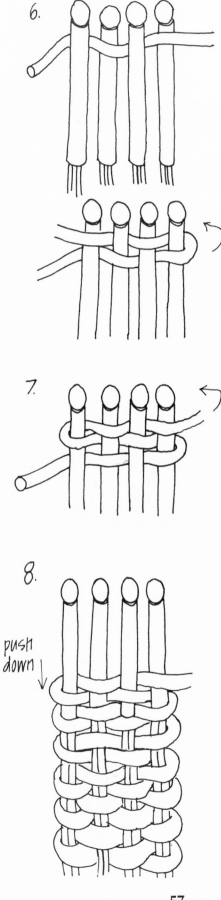

6.

7.

8.

push down ↓

Cloth

Spool Knitting

Spool knitting or "horsetails" is an old favorite. In this activity a plastic bottle with four cut prongs replaces the usual spool and nails, and a ball of fat **T-Shirt Yarn** (see page 21) is used instead or ordinary yarn.

Out of the center of the "spool" will grow a long tail of closely knit yarn. The tail can be coiled and stitched into an oval potholder or mat. Or it can be used as a door snake simply by laying it out along the bottom of a door or window to block the draft.

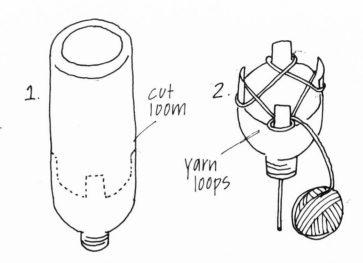

1. cut loom

2. yarn loops

MATERIALS

Plastic bottle about 2 inches in diameter (shampoo bottles are about the right size
T-Shirt Yarn
Thread for stitching coils (optional)

TOOLS

Scissors
Knitting needle or fat crochet hook
Sewing needle for stitching coils (optional)

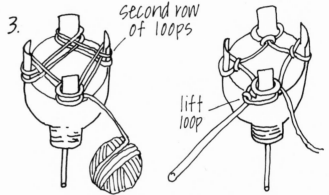

3. second row of loops

lift loop

HERE'S HOW

1. Cut off the bottom of the bottle. You don't need it. Then cut four big prongs out of the cut edge that are the same distance from one another.
2. Hold the "spool" upside down. Stick one end of a ball of T-Shirt Yarn down through the center so that it dangles an inch below the spool. Loop the yarn around the first prong, then around the other three. Push down the loops.
3. Make a second row of loops. With the knitting needle or crochet hook, lift the first loop on each prong up over the second loop, then release it. Once around is the first stitch. Tug on the dangling end of yarn to tighten it. After a number of go-arounds, a knitted tube of yarn will peep out from the bottom of the spool.
4. Make the knitted tube or tail as long as you like. To finish it off, snip off the yarn, leaving an extra 4 inches. Lift off each stitch from its prong in turn, inserting the yarn end. When they're all off, knot the yarn end through the last stitch loop.
5. You now have a finished door snake. If you like, stitch on a forked tongue cut out of felt for an added effect. Or you can coil the tail into a flat shape and stitch the coils in place. The length of the tail will determine whether you can make a potholder or a mat.

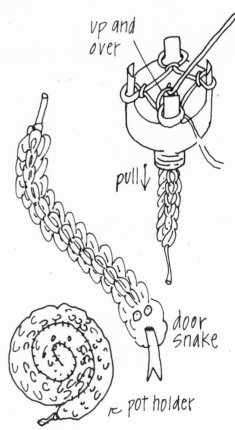

up and over

pull ↓

door snake

pot holder

Big Dummies

People have been making dummies for a long time. The straw man, the maid of spring, the queen of the May, and effigies are all examples. Scarecrows pop up every spring in gardens all over America, though birds seem to laugh at them. Making life-sized humanoids is a good chance for kids to exercise their talent for sculpture. A simple way to make dummies is to stuff some throwaway clothing. Garage sales, secondhand stores, and rag bags are good sources for materials. Halloween is the best time to stuff up a whole porch full of these weirdos.

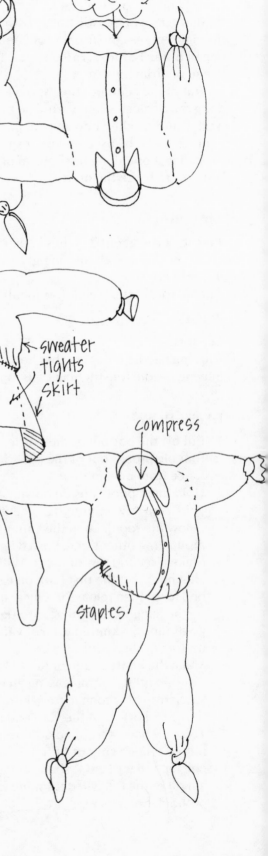

MATERIALS

Long-sleeved shirt or sweater
Pair of pants or tights
Newspaper
Paper lunch bag
6-inch length of stick (about the thickness of a
  broomstick)
String
Shoes, socks, gloves, hats, wigs, eyeglasses, or
  other accessories

TOOLS

Stapler, or needle and thread
Paint or markers
Scissors

HERE'S HOW

1. Knot the ends of the sleeves and the pants legs. Zip and button clothing closed.
2. Wad up heaps of newspaper and stuff it into the body and the pants or tights.
3. Stitch or staple the legs to the body. The stitching does not have to be fancy.
4. At this point you might need to compress the stuffing and add a bit more to make the figure solid.

5. Make the head. Stuff a paper lunch bag with paper. Insert the stick and tie it off to make the neck.
6. Poke the head into position and hold it in place with stitches or staples.
7. Add features, eyeglasses, hat, and mustache to complete the head of the big dummy. Feel free to try out whatever strikes your fancy.
8. Finish dressing the dummy with shoes, socks, vest, and sweater, or whatever else seems right.
9. Set up the sculpture somewhere where it can have a good view of what's going on.

stuff

tie

glue on ears

draw features

paste on feathers

wig

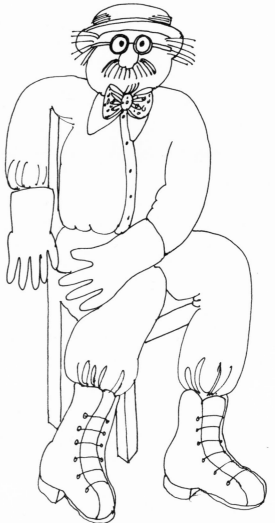

Dummy Dress

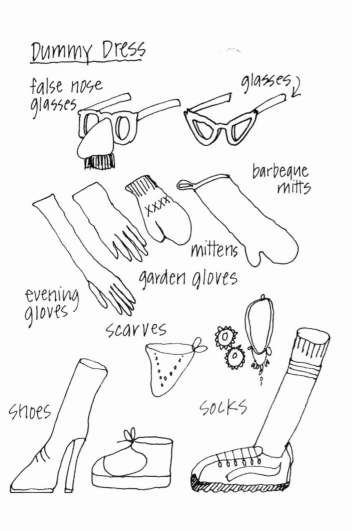

false nose glasses

glasses

barbeque mitts

mittens

garden gloves

evening gloves

scarves

shoes

socks

HERMAN THE HITCHHIKING DUMMY

Strictly speaking Herman the Hitchhiking dummy is not the trashy sort. As far as we know he wasn't even cut out of scrap, but his story does illustrate that dummies can go a long way.

Herman was cut from a sheet of plywood and stands over six feet tall. He is dressed in overalls that say San Francisco on the front pocket. The most obvious thing about him is his thumb which extends well out into the road. This thumb has managed to get him halfway across the country, which is quite a feat for someone who doesn't talk.

Herman is the creation of Robert Foster of Evergreen, Colorado, who made him, addressed him to his friend Michael Leydon of Menlo Park, California, and set him beside the road. The only luggage that Herman carried was a bunch of preaddressed postcards. These cards marked his progress as his drivers mailed them home. They reported that Herman attended parties, met all sorts of friendly people, appeared on T.V., and was detained for hitchhiking and vagrancy. He got as far west as San Bruno, just 16 miles from his destination when he disappeared. Speculations were that Herman might have been abducted by the Plywood Liberation Organization or perhaps some splinter organization. Offers of rewards failed and his whereabouts remain a mystery. Finally, Robert Foster gave up hope and made Herman II at the beginning of the summer. He left him by the side of the road just before the Fourth of July.

Herman II had better luck than his predecessor. He arrived at "Uncle" Michael's house in Menlo Park a couple of weeks later, delivered by a couple driving from Kansas. Despite the warm welcome, Herman II had little to say about his adventures.

Stuffed Drawings

Here is a way to make art that looks good enough to squeeze. Any kid can make a drawing on cloth and stuff it. These plump, squishy drawings are good to use as beanbags or hang as decorations. Make a whole colony of people from outer space. Stick pins in one and call it a pin cushion. Put perfume behind its ears and stick it in a dresser drawer to scent clothes.

MATERIALS

White or light-colored cloth (Old sheets are perfect.)
Crayons, fabric crayons, or felt markers
Sheet of paper
Stuffing (cotton or synthetic)

TOOLS

Iron (and a surface to iron on)
Scissors
Needle and thread, or stapler

HERE'S HOW

1. Make a drawing on the fabric.
2. If you used crayons, lay a sheet of paper over the drawing and press it with a warm iron.
3. Cut out the picture leaving a ½-inch margin all around.
4. Cut another piece of fabric exactly the same shape. Use another color cloth if you want to be fancy.
5. Put the two pieces of cloth together with the drawing facing inward.
6. Stitch or staple all around the drawing, leaving a small section open. Do this leaving a ½-inch margin.
7. Trim the margin to ¼ inch as shown.
8. Turn the drawing right side out.
9. Add the stuffing through the opening.
10. Sew or staple the opening closed.

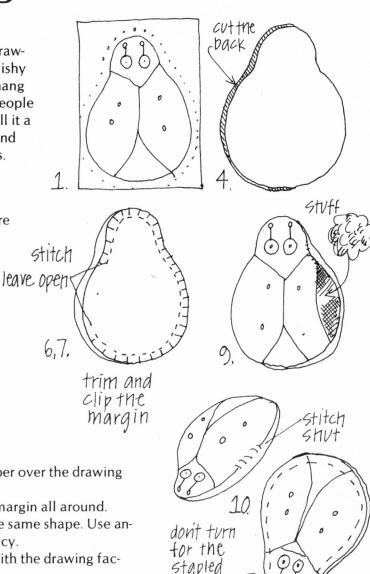

Leaf Prints

Decorating a cloth with a hammer? That's right. It does sound like something that a lunatic might do, but it works. Wonderful impressions of leaves can be pounded onto cloth with a hammer. And if that doesn't sound crazy enough, there's a dip in a vat of rusty water to dye the cloth. It's an old Japanese way of printing with plants. The basic materials are some scraps of sheets and some rusty metal—and, of course, some leaves.

MATERIALS

Water
Rusty metal
Newspaper
Leaves (Not all leaves work well. Leaves with lots of tannins are best. You will have to experiment.)
White fabric (Old sheets work wonderfully.)

TOOLS

Bucket
Spoon
Scissors
Hammer (and a smooth, hard surface to hammer on)
Iron (and a surface to iron on)

HERE'S HOW TO MAKE THE RUSTY DYEBATH

1. Fill a bucket with water. If you are working with small bits of fabric, a quart of dyebath will be enough. If you are planning to do bigger things like T-shirts, you will need at least a gallon of water to start with.
2. Gather up all the rusty metal bits you can find. Scrape the rust onto a sheet of newspaper.
3. Grind the rusty scrapings into powder with the back of a spoon.
4. Stir the rust into the water. There should be enough rust to make a rich color.

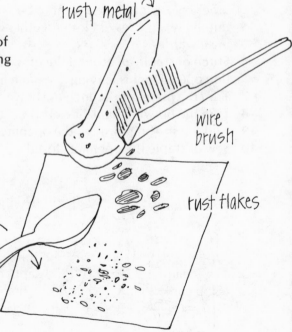

rusty metal

wire brush

rust flakes

press the flakes into powder

HERE'S HOW TO PRINT

1. Choose your leaf. Lay it on a smooth, hard surface, such as a block of wood or smooth concrete.
2. Cut a square of fabric larger than the leaf. Lay it over the leaf.
3. Holding the fabric smooth with one hand, carefully begin tapping with the hammer. You should see the shape of the leaf come through the fabric. Keep tapping until you get a good impression.
4. Peel away the leaf.
5. Soak the cloth in a bucket of water until it is really wet. This should prevent streaking in the rusty dyebath.
6. Dip the cloth in the dyebath. Let the rusty color soak into the cloth. The longer you let it soak, the more yellow the cloth will become, and the darker the leaf design.
7. Hang it out to dry in the sun.
8. Press the leaf print with a warm iron.
9. Mount it if you like.

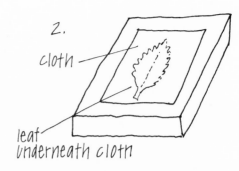

2.
cloth
leaf underneath cloth

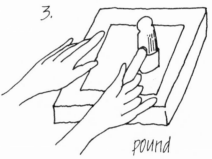

3.
pound

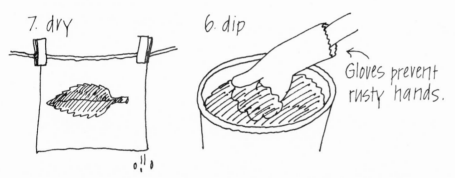

7. dry

6. dip

Gloves prevent rusty hands.

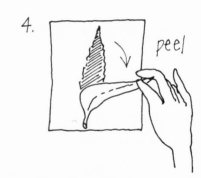

4.
peel

Notes: If you can't find enough old rusty stuff, use a little artificial rust, which is also known as ferrous sulphate. It comes in a powder and is available from a chemical supplier for very little money. A half-pound will make a number of dyebaths and should cost less than $2.00. Just add this powder to water to make a rusty dyebath.

Order ferrous sulphate by mail if it isn't available locally. Write: Straw into Gold, 5533 College Ave., Oakland, California 94618, for their current prices.

Not all leaves will work. Some don't contain enough tannins to react with the rust to make the design permanent. The best seasons for this project are the summer and early fall when the leaves are still juicy but developed. Some leaves, like pine needles, will work anytime. They are best picked after a hot spell and not after a rain. Scarves or T-shirts can be printed with this technique.

Pound the cloth on a smooth surface or the cloth will tear.

Leaf prints can be made without the dyebath step. You will make a nice impression that will disappear when you wash the cloth. You can even try this pounding method on paper—gently!

Wild Weavings

The mesh sacks that hold 50 pounds of potatoes or onions make a good base for wild weavings. Those big holes are just begging to be threaded with hanks of colored yarns, single strands of **T-Shirt Yarn** (see page 21), or all sorts of odds and ends. Try twigs, plant parts, or sticks of rolled-up paper for a really crazy weaving.

MATERIALS

Mesh bags (Ask for 50-pound onion or potato bags from the produce department at the market. They usually come in red or purple.)
Plastic bottle
Something to weave with (Try assorted yarns, ribbons, or fabric strips, or odds and ends like plant stems, or straws.)
Straw or stick
String

TOOLS

Scissors
Ruler
Paper punch
Plastic needle (Make this from the plastic bottle.)

HERE'S HOW

1. Cut a piece of mesh the size you want the weaving to be. A long, skinny piece (about 4 inches by 12 inches) is good to start with.
2. Make a needle by cutting out the pattern from a flat piece of plastic bottle. Punch a hole for the eye.
3. Thread the needle with yarn.
4. Weave rows of colored yarns in and out across the strip. Feel free to skip lines, pull out threads, or add in straws and plant parts. Push holes in the mesh with your fingers. Do whatever feels right.
5. When you are finished, weave a straw or a stick across the top.
6. Tie a string to both ends of the stick.
7. Hang your wild weaving.

Notes: Try weaving a picture instead of a design. Or make a drawstring bag. Cut the sack off from the top around the label. Weave a nylon cord around the top and bottom. Knot the bottom closed and use the top cord as a drawstring.

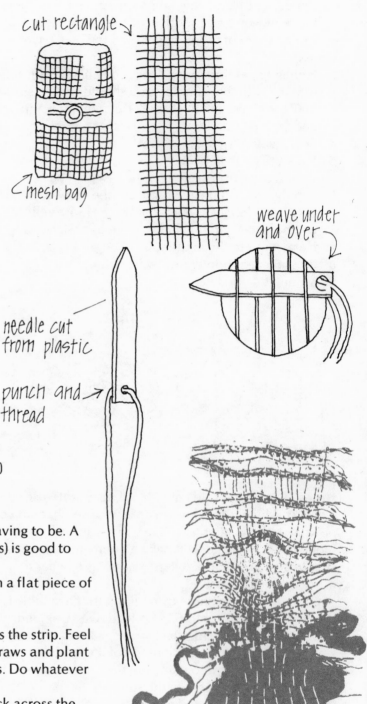

cut rectangle

mesh bag

weave under and over

needle cut from plastic

punch and thread

JOE BELL'S WINDMILLS

Some people call them wind-spinners, pin-wheels, or whirligigs. Joe Bell calls them wind-mills. He should know because he is an expert at making windmills. It all started one day at home in Staunton, Virginia, when he was fooling around with some can lids. He stuck them on a piece of wood. He took his creation outdoors and it started spinning like crazy.

One construction led to another until Joe had made an entire yard full of wind machines from scrap materials. Some are 30 feet high with more than 30 spinners on each one. He uses bits of tin, slats from old venetian blinds, and scrap wood. He paints his spinners with bright stripes and polka dots.

Of course a yard full of brightly painted spinners attracts attention, so it wasn't too long before collectors and dealers started buying Joe's windmills. Now he's in the business of making trash art.

Adapted from
Contemporary American Folk Artists,
Elinor L. Horowitz, Lippincott, 1975.

Wands

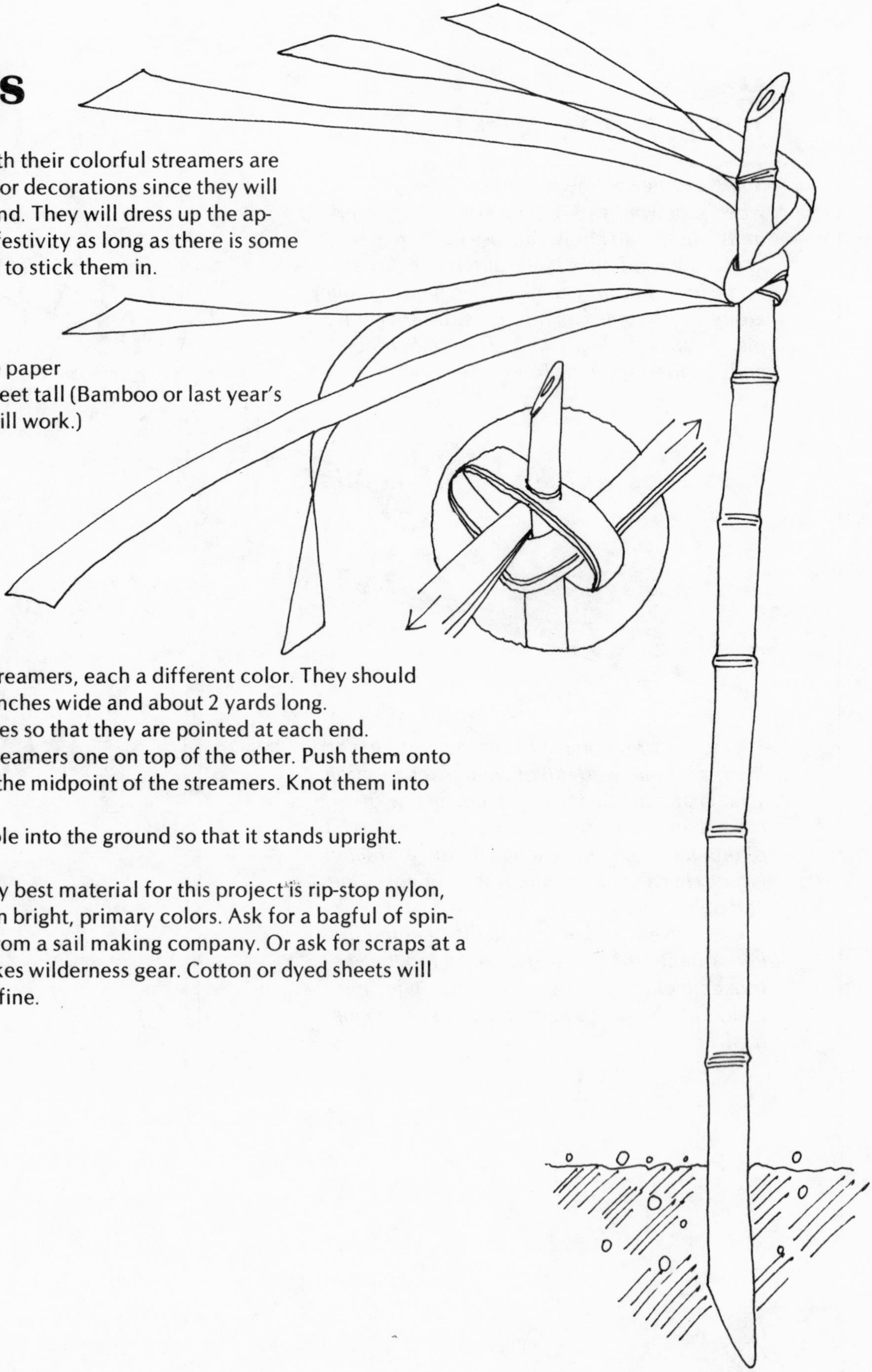

These poles with their colorful streamers are good for outdoor decorations since they will rustle in the wind. They will dress up the approach to any festivity as long as there is some earth or a lawn to stick them in.

MATERIALS

Fabric or crepe paper
Poles about 6 feet tall (Bamboo or last year's beanpoles will work.)

TOOLS

Scissors
Yardstick
Small saw

HERE'S HOW

1. Cut three streamers, each a different color. They should measure 2 inches wide and about 2 yards long.
2. Saw the poles so that they are pointed at each end.
3. Hold the streamers one on top of the other. Push them onto the pole at the midpoint of the streamers. Knot them into position.
4. Stick the pole into the ground so that it stands upright.

Notes: The very best material for this project is rip-stop nylon, which comes in bright, primary colors. Ask for a bagful of spinnaker scraps from a sail making company. Or ask for scraps at a place that makes wilderness gear. Cotton or dyed sheets will also work just fine.

Rings

Like the wands, these rings look wonderful blowing in a breeze. Hang them outdoors from eaves or trees. Or string them up indoors from the ceiling.

MATERIALS

Plastic lid
Fabric or crepe paper
String

TOOLS

Pointed scissors
Yardstick
String

HERE'S HOW

1. Cut the center out of the plastic lid, leaving only a ring.
2. Cut a number of colorful streamers about a yard long.
3. Slip knot them onto the ring.
4. Tie a string around the lid rim opposite the streamers.
5. Hang it.

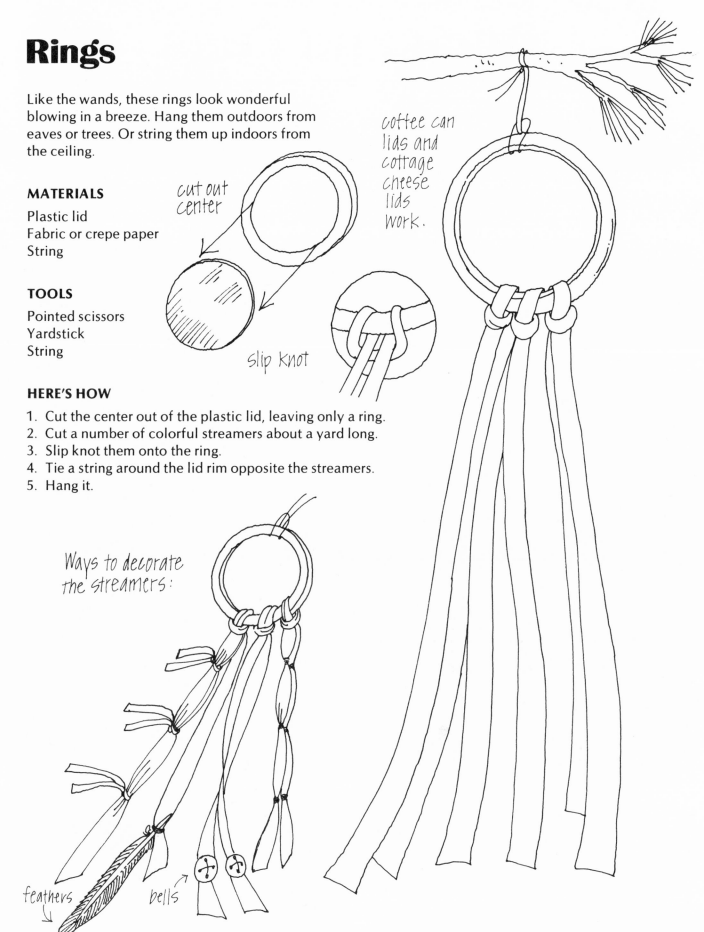

cut out center

Slip knot

coffee can lids and cottage cheese lids work.

Ways to decorate the streamers:

feathers

bells

Odds and Ends

Pick-Up Pictures

This is the perfect project to do on an excursion. A beach with lots of flotsam and jetsam washed up on the shore is ideal for pick-up pictures, but there are plenty of other places to find the materials for such a work of art. Look in places like a street after a parade, a parking lot around a supermarket, vacant lots, and gutters.

MATERIALS

White glue
Cardboard or wooden slab
Found bits and pieces (Use bones, sticks, stones, bottle caps, plastic bits, string, fragments of glass, seeds, and shells.)

HERE'S HOW

1. Take a walk in a spot where you are bound to find things.
2. Pick up something interesting like a gnarled stick, a stone, or a glittery piece of broken glass. Ask yourself what it looks like.
3. Find some other things to use along with it to make a picture.
4. Lay out the pick-up pieces on the ground. Add more parts, letting your imagination and the stuff close at hand be your guide. Things like faces are fun to do.
5. If you want to take your pick-up picture home to enjoy later, glue it on a slab of wood or cardboard with white glue.

Notes: Sometimes a trash artist leaves a work of this kind lying right where it was created on the beach, on the sidewalk, or in a vacant lot. Part of the fun is wondering if other people noticed it and what they thought of it.

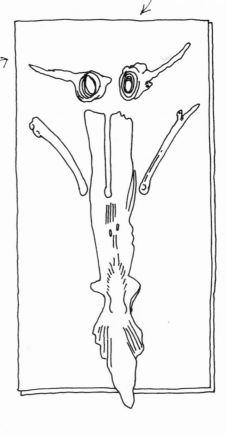

cardboard back

assemble with glue

Sawdust Dough

Sawdust dough has been a favorite recipe of scout leaders, camp counselors, and veteran arts-and-crafters for a long time. It is a lot of fun dipping into the woody-smelling, gooey mass and modeling heads, primitive animals, or mad machinery. The dough dries a blond color and has a rough texture which can be sanded smooth and painted, or left natural.

MATERIALS

Sawdust (Look for this under a table saw at a lumberyard or a cabinet shop.)
Wheat paste
Water
Tempera paint

TOOLS

Sieve or screen
Container (like a big coffee can)
Measuring cup
Stirrer
Heavy cardboard or wooden slab
Sandpaper
Paintbrush

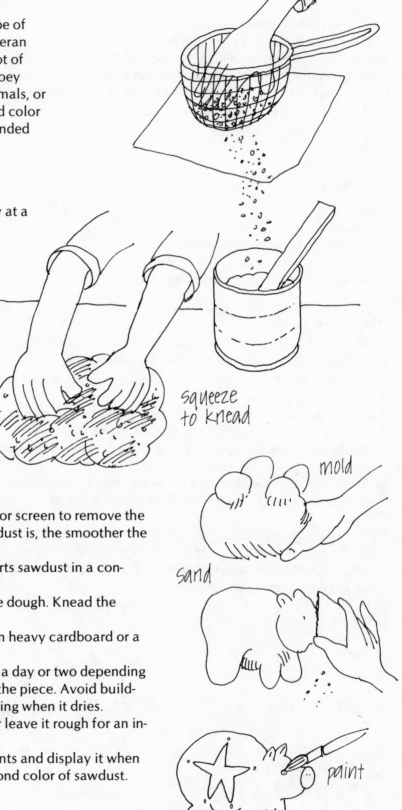

squeeze to knead

mold

sand

paint

HERE'S HOW

1. Strain the sawdust through the sieve or screen to remove the big lumps and chunks. The finer the dust is, the smoother the clay will be.
2. Mix one part wheat paste to three parts sawdust in a container.
3. Add enough water to make a claylike dough. Knead the dough to make it smooth.
4. Shape and sculpt the dough. Work on heavy cardboard or a wooden slab.
5. Let your sculpture dry. This will take a day or two depending on the weather and the thickness of the piece. Avoid building anything too fat to prevent cracking when it dries.
6. Sand the sawdust dough sculpture or leave it rough for an interesting texture.
7. Paint the sculpture with tempera paints and display it when the paint has dried, or leave it the blond color of sawdust.

Half Masks

Kids can cut out a pair of eye-bulging goggles from an egg carton that will totally change their looks. There are six sets of goggles waiting to be cut out of every egg carton and each pair can be custom-designed. And there are even more possibilities for inventive nose masks.

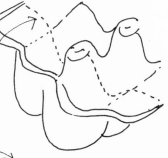

cut along the dotted line

punch holes

MATERIALS

Egg cartons (any kind—pulp, Styrofoam, or flats)
String
Poster paint

add ties

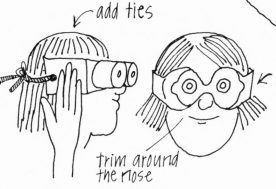

TOOLS

Scissors
Paper punch
A helper
Paintbrush

Cut eye holes

trim around the nose

other versions:

HERE'S HOW

1. Cut out a pair of egg cups. Think of them as goggles. Let their shape help you decide how to cut.
2. Hold them up to your face to see how they fit. Trim them so they fit against your nose and rest comfortably on your face.
3. Punch a hole on either side. Insert ties to hold the mask on.
4. Get someone to help you mark where the eye hole should go in each cup.
5. Cut out the eyes. There are a couple of ways to do this. Try cutting slits, or punching a lot of little holes, or cutting out two big holes.
6. Decorate the mask with paint.

Notes: There are a lot of ways to cut a half mask. Look at the illustrations for some hints. Or try cutting out a single cup for a nose mask. Add some string to tie it on and perhaps a mustache. An alternative to using egg cartons is to use the pulp sheets that hold fruit in packing boxes. Get those from the grocery store.

cups cut from fruit packing
nail holes

egg carton nose masks

Odds and Ends Prints

This project is a junk classic and for good reason. Making prints from commonplace objects can be lots of fun, and the results can be quite stunning. Seeing the surfaces of everyday stuff translated into different shapes and patterns is an exciting experience in itself. There are several ways to print with odds and ends, but the materials are basically the same. With this method you print with each object directly. Thicker objects work best here because fingers stay farther away from the inky surface, and smudging is less of a problem.

MATERIALS

Odds and ends (kitchen utensils; bits of hardware like nuts, bolts, and washers; blocks of wood; tinker toys; plastic caps)
Printer's ink or thick poster paint (Use water soluble printer's ink and save yourself a permanent mess.)
Sheets of paper (Absorbent paper, such as newsprint, works best.)

TOOLS

Ink roller
Plate or cookie sheet (or some flat surface on which to roll the ink)

HERE'S HOW

1. Roll out a splash of ink, coating the roller.
2. Roll ink onto the surface you want to print.
3. Carefully press the inky surface onto the paper.
4. Repeat the process to make a design.

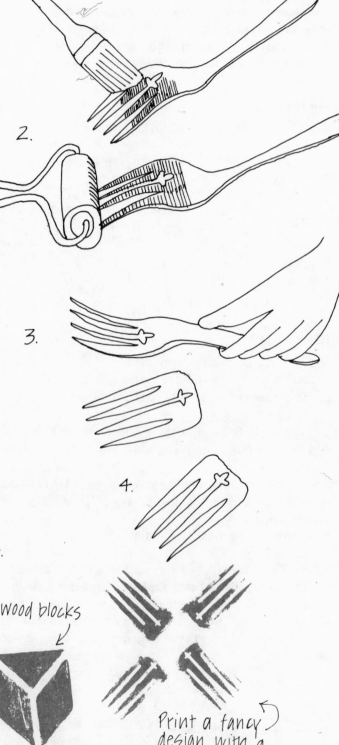

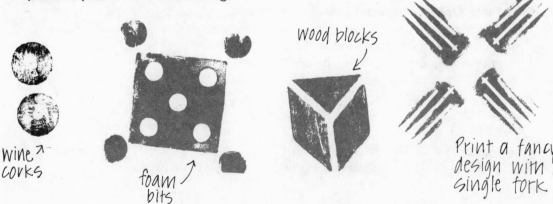

wine corks

foam bits

wood blocks

Print a fancy design with a single fork.

Odds and Ends Block

For this method you need to make a cardboard block to print with. This way is best if you want a design using an assortment of odds and ends. It is also a good way to handle thin things like coins and pins that are hard to ink and print without leaving awful smears all over the page.

MATERIALS

Odds and ends (washers, bobby pins, paper clips, wire, bottle caps, seeds, or any other thin assortment)
Cardboard
Glue
Printer's ink or thick poster paint (Use water soluble printer's ink.)
Sheets of paper (Absorbent paper like news-print works best.)

TOOLS

Scissors
Ink roller
Plate or cookie sheet (or some flat surface on which to roll the ink)

HERE'S HOW

1. Assemble your odds and ends in a design you like. The only rule is that the assorted junk must be the same thickness.
2. Cut a square of cardboard to accommodate the design.
3. Arrange your odds and ends on the cardboard. Glue them into position. Let them dry.
4. Roll out a splash of ink, coating the roller.
5. Ink the odds and ends block by coating the odds and ends with the ink from the roller.
6. Print it.

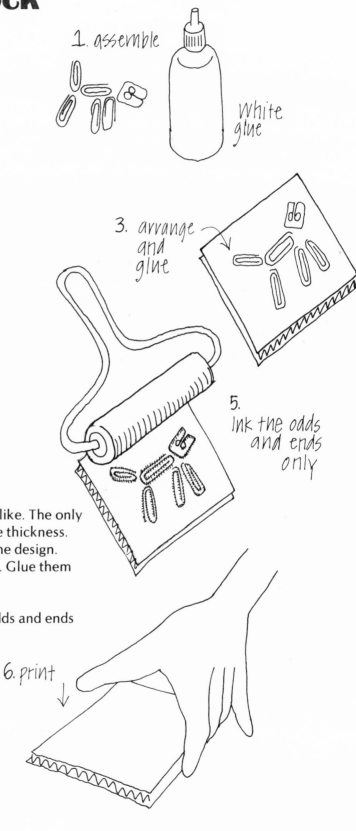

1. assemble

white glue

3. arrange and glue

5. Ink the odds and ends only

6. print

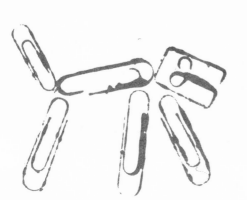

BOTTLE GARDEN

In the town of Golden, New Mexico, there is a little yard that glitters in the sun with jewellike colors of green, blue, brown, and clear crystals. It is Adell Scartaccini's garden of bottles. There are pickle jars, old medicine bottles, wine bottles, broken bits of bottles, and electrical insulators. They are strung along the wire fence and stuck in the earth. They sprout from a tree and nestle in the shrubs, and there is a bottle orchestra that plays in the wind.

All of this glass is not just extravagance. Adell's garden is partly watered by the moisture that is trapped in the upturned bottles by condensation. The glass also acts as an effective heat collector, raising the temperature among the growing things — like a greenhouse.

Adell's favorite bottles are the rare hand-blown ones, but she uses all kinds. She is especially fond of the cobalt blue ones that aren't made anymore. Some of the folks in Golden seem to have taken a special interest in Adell's sparkling garden. Sometimes Adell will find that friends and neighbors have left more bottles at her garden gate to help her garden grow.

Adapted from
Wizard's Eye, Charles Milligan
and Jim Higgs, Chronicle Books, 1978.

Window Pane Prints

The art printed on a window pane is one-of-a-kind. Since only one copy of a design can be made from the original, it is a good way to work for kids who get bored easily or who like to draw a lot. Old panes of glass, which can often be found lying around garages or companies that replace windows, are best for this project. Old mirrors, sheets of Plexiglas, or picture frames with the glass intact will also work. Use any flat, sturdy, smooth surface.

MATERIALS

Printer's ink (Use water soluble printer's ink.)
Sheets of paper

TOOLS

Ink roller
Window pane
Things to draw with (Try eraser ends, pencils, sticks, and combs, or cut your own tools from a plastic bottle.)

HERE'S HOW

1. Squirt a line of ink onto the window.
2. Spread it out evenly with the roller.
3. Draw a design in the ink with a tool. Try different sorts of tools.
4. When you are satisfied with your design, carefully press a sheet of paper onto the ink. Smooth it down, trying not to smear it around.
5. Pull away the design.
6. Reink the window pane. Repeat the process for the next design.
7. Let the design dry. This ink is thick and sticky so it may take a few hours.

Notes: You might want to try cutting your own drawing tools from a plastic bottle or plastic lids. Experiment with combs, pointy tools, and broad flat ones.

1. window pane · ink

2. roll ink

3. draw a design

4. smooth down

5. peel away

7. let the print dry

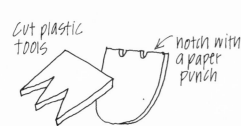

Cut plastic tools — notch with a paper punch

Found Tools: bottle top

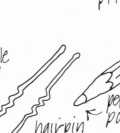

hairpin · pencil point and end

Pencil Stub Tops

This is a simple way to make a classic toy from scrap materials. Everybody generally has a collection of old pencil stubs that are the result of a lot of writer's cramp. Kids can search for them in the bottoms of pencil holders and in the backs of desk drawers. Besides being fun to spin, the tops are great for exploring the secrets of color-mixing and creating some optical illusions.

MATERIALS

Corrugated cardboard
Pencil stubs
Paper clips
Stiff paper
Glue
Magazines

TOOLS

Circle pattern or pencil compass
Scissors
Mat knife
Pencil sharpener

HERE'S HOW

1. Cut out a 3½-inch circle from cardboard. Use a compass or circle pattern to make sure that it is perfectly round.
2. Score a cross at the exact center with a mat knife.
3. Sharpen the pencil stub to about 2½ to 3 inches.
4. Push the pencil through the center of the circle.
5. Give your pencil stub top a trial spin. Hold the pencil upright between your thumb and index fingers, and give it a twirl.
6. Adjust your top so that it doesn't wobble. Do this by raising or lowering the circle on the pencil. Make sure the circle is on straight. Weight the edge with paper clips for stability.
7. Add a drop of glue to hold the circle in position on the pencil.
8. Cut a circle from a printed magazine page. Slip it onto the top and give it a whirl. See what happens when you spin it.

Notes: Try cutting circles out of all sorts of different magazine pages. Or try coloring some circles to spin. Cut them from gift paper and experiment by coloring them different ways.

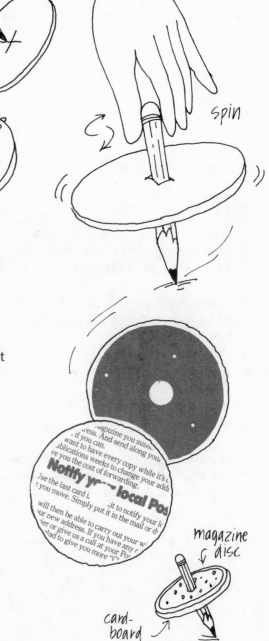

Egg Grenades

These confetti-filled concoctions are made just to break. They're fun for a special occasion like April Fool's Day, New Year's Eve, or a bon voyage party.

MATERIALS

Eggs
Paper (Magazine pages or scraps are fine.)
Tape or rubber cement
Felt markers

TOOLS

Pointed scissors
Bowl

HERE'S HOW

1. First empty the egg of its raw insides. Do this by holding the fat end of the egg toward you. Carefully poke a hole in the shell with the tip of some scissors. Slide the blade in to break the yolk. Shake the contents out into the bowl. Rinse the eggshell with cool water. Let it dry.
2. Cut a sheet of paper into little bits of confetti. Quarter-inch squares are a good size. Or use the dots that collect around a paper punch.
3. Fill the egg with the paper confetti.
4. Seal up the open end with a piece of tape. Or cut a square of paper as shown in the illustration. Stick it in place with some rubber cement.
5. Decorate the outside of the shell.
6. Throw the egg grenade so that all the confetti spills out. The best way to do this is to peel off the seal and crack the egg in half. Then toss it up in the air so the bits of paper spill everywhere.

Notes: Egg grenade throwers should be on the alert so that they know when scrambled eggs or omelettes are being prepared. It is the perfect opportunity to collect a supply of eggshells.

Card Architecture

Playing cards with only part of a deck is about as much fun as swimming with shoes on. But the cards can be used to build something. Kids can combine that crippled deck with a handful of plastic soda straws and become card architects.

MATERIALS

Deck of cards
Plastic straws

TOOLS

Scissors
Ruler

HERE'S HOW

1. Cut the straws into 2-inch lengths.
2. Cut a slit into each end. These are the connectors.
3. Get out the cards and build a structure using the cards as the walls and the straws as the connectors.

Note: Another method for using cards as building materials is to cut slits as illustrated.

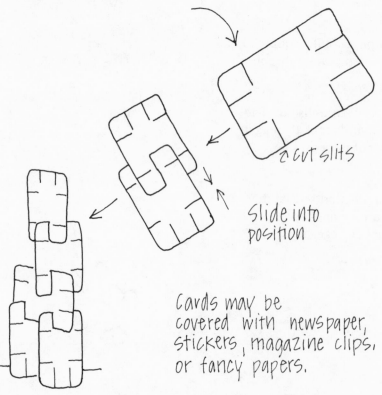

cut slits

2 cut slits

Slide into position

Cards may be covered with newspaper, stickers, magazine clips, or fancy papers.

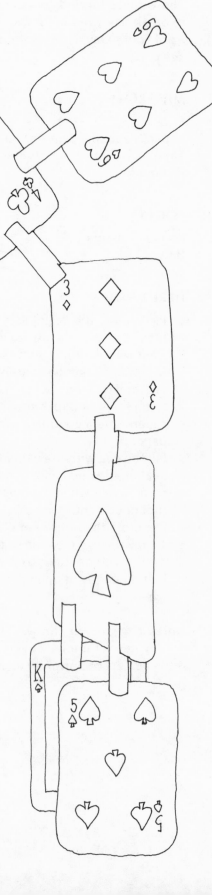

Foiled Pins

Here's a way to make a pin that looks a lot like antique silver. The secret is aluminum foil and some elbow grease. The same method can be used to make a belt buckle, a medal, or a whole suit of armor.

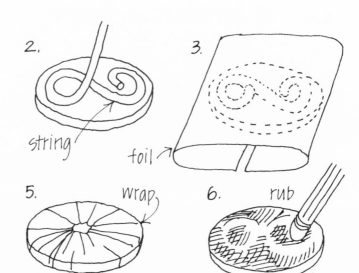

MATERIALS

Lightweight cardboard
White glue
String of various thicknesses
Aluminum foil (Heavy duty is best.)
India ink, or black tempera mixed with liquid detergent
Pin backs

TOOLS

Scissors
Eraser
Paintbrush
Steel wool

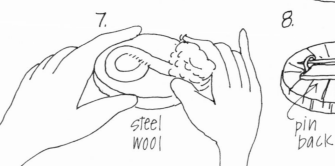

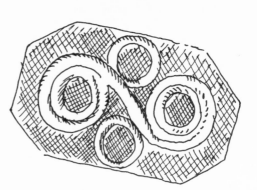

HERE'S HOW

1. Cut the shape of your pin out of cardboard. Keep it simple.
2. Coat one side of the cardboard with glue. Lay out the string on it in a design that you like. The string will show up later as a ridge under the foil surface.
3. Cut a piece of foil. Make it big enough to wrap around the cardboard so that no cardboard shows on the back.
4. Coat the dull side of the foil with glue. Then stick it to the string side of the cardboard.
5. Wrap the foil around to cover the back. Rub the back so that the foil lies flat.
6. Rub the front of the pin to bring up the texture. Use something smooth like the eraser end of a pencil and take care not to tear the foil.
7. Paint the front with black ink or paint. A squirt of liquid detergent will help the paint stick to the slick foil. Let it dry.
8. Rub the front of the pin with steel wool to shine up the string ridges.
9. Glue on the pin back.
10. Coat the front and back with a layer of white glue.

CARPENTER THE CARPENTER

Miles Carpenter has made twisty snakes 20 feet long, devils, dogs, pies with blackbirds inside, and larger-than-life watermelons. He uses all kinds of wood, but one of his favorite materials is roots — gnarled, bumpy, lumpy roots that he finds or digs up.

The trick is to look at these tangled pieces and see something in them. Then you just bring it out of the wood. For Miles, that means carving and painting his wood works. He has been working with wood all his life, but it wasn't until he retired from the sawmill that he took up carving in a serious way.

It was a giant watermelon that Miles carved to draw attention to his fruit stand in Waverly, Virginia, that got him his first recognition as a genuine artist. A man from a museum offered to buy it for $150. That watermelon is now at home in New York's Abbey Aldrich Rockefeller Museum of Folk Art. Miles Carpenter has carved another.

Adapted from
Contemporary American Folk Artists,
Elinor L. Horowitz, Lippincott, 1975.

Stretcher Bars

Stretcher bars are an artist's trick for framing art on fabric. Here is a way to do it that won't cost a nickel. The basic materials are from crates that have wooden frame ends. Fruit markets usually throw away melon or tomato crates, which are the right kind for making stretcher bars. This kind of three dimensional frame can be used to display any fabric or paper artwork.

MATERIALS

Wooden frame (from a melon or tomato crate with wooden ends)
Piece of fabric art (at least 4 inches bigger all around than the frame)
Wire

TOOLS

Hammer and small tacks, or a staple gun

HERE'S HOW

1. Knock the crate apart with a hammer. It's okay to bash up the sides but leave the wooden ends intact.
2. Put the artwork face down on a clean surface. Position the frame on top of it.
3. Pull the two opposite sides of the fabric around the frame. Tack or staple them in position, pulling the fabric tight.
4. Make square corners.
5. Tack the opposte ends in place.
6. Add a wire to hang it from. Put it up. Step back and admire your work.

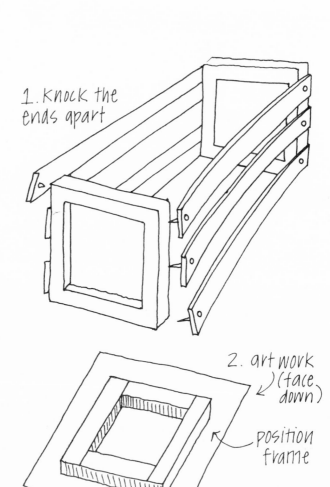

1. Knock the ends apart

2. art work (face down)

position frame

3. tack sides

4.

fold up

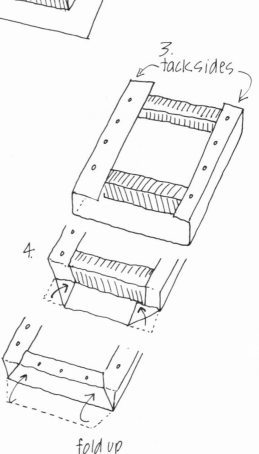

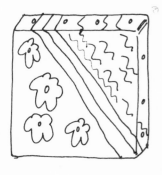

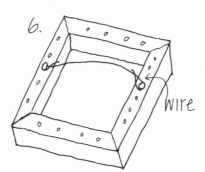

6.

wire

Wooden Frame

Use those same melon crate ends you used to make stretcher bars for a more traditional picture frame. Frame any piece of flat artwork that deserves hanging.

MATERIALS

Wooden frame (from a melon or tomato crate with wooden ends)
Artwork (about the size of the frame)
Cardboard
Tempera paint
Wire

TOOLS

Hammer and small tacks, or a staple gun
Scissors
Paintbrush

HERE'S HOW

1. Knock apart the box to get the wooden ends.
2. Carefully pry the cardboard backing from the wooden ends. Try to remove it without damaging it.
3. If you didn't succeed, cut a sheet of cardboard the same size as the frame.
4. Center the art in the frame.
5. Trim the artwork so that it is the same size as the cardboard.
6. Tack the cardboard back on so that the art faces out of the frame.
7. Consider painting the frame with a color or a design.
8. Add a wire to the back and hang up your masterpiece.

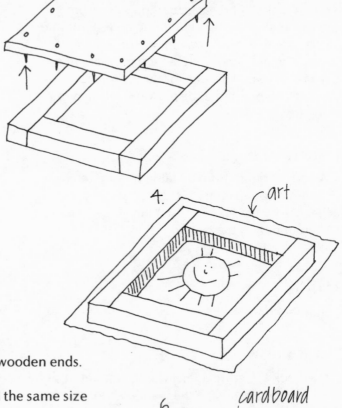

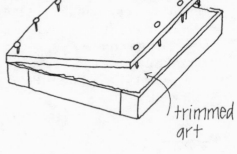

Wound-Up Wire Rings

These rings can be made from wire in less time than it takes to watch a TV program. They are made out of flexible copper wire that comes in bright, plastic coats of all colors. The phone company uses this wire and so do people who work with electronic equipment.

MATERIALS

Plastic-coated copper wire

TOOLS

Scissors
Ruler

HERE'S HOW

1. Cut a length of wire 12 inches long.
2. Smooth out the wiggles in the wire by running it through your fingers, stretching it as you go, or by running the piece back and forth along a table edge.
3. Circle your ring finger with wire. Make the circle about $1/8$ inch bigger than your finger.
4. Do this two more times so there are three circles side by side.
5. Twist the long end of the wire through the circle. Begin wrapping the circles. Continue wrapping all around.
6. If you run out of wire add some more as shown.
7. When the whole circle is wrapped, clip off the end and tuck it out of sight.

Notes: You can use different colors on the same ring. Try twisting on loops or even a flower if you like. The same method will produce a wound-up bracelet if you start with a hoop big enough to slip over your hand.

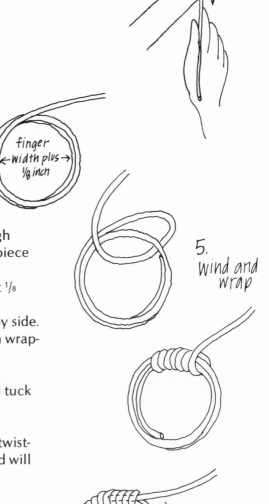

2.

4. finger width plus → $1/8$ inch

5. wind and wrap

6. Slide a new piece under the wraps and continue

Variations:

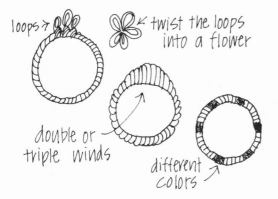

loops → twist the loops into a flower

double or triple winds

different colors

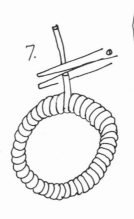

7.

Teacher Notes

Magazine Robots are a collage project. There are many ingenious ways to make a collage. Older kids might be interested in studying how some of the famous artists have done it. Send them off to the art history section in the library to bring back pictures for inspiration.

Nothing can be more frustrating than trying to force a dull pair of scissors across a sheet of cardboard. For projects like **Boomerangs** that require accurate cutting, it is best to give kids scissors that work well, with a warning to be careful. If they abuse a pair of good scissors, they deserve to be demoted to those miserable snub-nosed models.

Buried Pictures and **Comic Book Character and Super Hero Pins** are both decoupage projects. Handling small, cut-out pieces is difficult for little hands. Primary-age kids can make buried pictures if the scale is large enough (about the size of a coffee can). One variation is to have kids cut shapes from white or colored tape. Show them how to apply the shapes to a dark background, then coat the surface with glue.

The best way to dispense white glue is to pour small amounts of it into containers like baby food jars. Kids can use their fingers as spreaders if they are covering a small area. For large areas, use a brush. Any kid who has worked with white glue for five minutes will discover what fun it is to spread glue over his or her hands and to peel it off when it dries. You might want to warn your kids in advance: no glue mittens.

Fold-Up Boxes and **Ribands**—in fact, all projects that require careful folding and following directions—are best for children in fourth grade and up. Learn the process yourself. Show the kids the finished product and proceed one step at a time. Make sure to catch all the stragglers before proceeding to the next step. You might station a couple of the classroom's fold-up wizards around the room to help the kids who have trouble. It may be slow going, but once kids get it, expect to see dozens and dozens of those fold-up projects all year long.

Strip Papier Mâché, on a big scale, is a long-term project. Older children will have no problem handling the drying periods and coming back to the project later. Divide kids into small groups if you make a large animal like a dinosaur—one for the head, the legs, the tail, and a group to do the painting.

Primary children are happiest with more immediate results. **Papier Mâché Clay** is better for them. A few drops of wintergreen oil added to the modeling compound will make it last longer in the wet stage.

Kids of all ages love making **Marbelous Gift Bags.** Marbling is magic. Primary kids are happy just doing it. Older children will want to apply the marbling process to sheets of paper in order to make beautiful gift wrap, book covers, or stationery.

If you need a project to fascinate everyone from kindergarten to college, **Amazing Shrinking Tops** are the answer. Bring a toaster oven to class so your junk artists can see the magic shrinking process firsthand. If you have to use your home oven, you need to do a little homework. Decorate a lid in class. Give everyone a good look. Then take it home and shrink it. Show it to the kids the next day. Enthusiasm will be rampant. Try to have a set of felt markers for every three artists.

The best part about **Foam Boats** is putting them on water. If at all possible, plan an excursion so that the foam boat builders can test their ships for seaworthiness. Discuss a way to power the fleet.

Squirt Pictures can be extended in a mathematical direction with a discussion of symmetry. Squirt paintings are a fine example of bilateral symmetry. Another fold at right angles to the first will show radial symmetry. With a bit of practice you can create some handsome bisymmetrical butterflies. Hang a flock of them from the ceiling with threads. They look sensational fluttering around in the breeze.

When making **Plastic Sandwiches,** or any project that requires an iron, you might want to check your school's wiring. In older buildings, plugging in that second iron may well put out the lights. This won't make you popular with the class next door that is in the middle of a film. An older child or adult should be in charge of the iron.

Stuffed Drawings provide a good way to introduce some needle and thread techniques to older kids. For younger kids you will need an adult with a sewing machine on standby to do the stitching process. Staples are an even better method to use with younger kids. A good variation is to make stuffed drawings on paper. First draw on paper, cut out a front and back, staple the edges, and stuff the pocket with wads of paper. Try this with any size drawing—even life-size tracings of kids on newsprint.

Odds and Ends Prints and **Odds and Ends Block** have an enormous tactile appeal. Plenty of paper is advisable so that the kids can practice making clean prints. Keep a bucket of water on hand to toss the printers in. This will save some clean up time.

Window Pane Prints are possible on any smooth, slick surface. Formica table tops or sink cutouts will work wonderfully. One teacher had an entire class working at long tables substituting tempera for printer's ink. The kids loved it.

The **Pencil Stub Tops** require some fine tuning. Make sure all the parts are as symmetrical as possible before they are assembled. Some fine coordination is necessary to get them to spin, so these are best for third grade and up.

Once in a while, on the right occasion, a little controlled rowdiness is good for everyone. **Egg Grenades** are pretty harmless. Save them for a special event, and warn the custodian. They should prove to be a great money-maker at the school carnival.

Card Architecture appeals to kids of all ages. Fourth graders and older kids will use them in more elaborate constructions. You can make the sets fancier by spray painting the cards with gold or colored paint. Stash these sets in a can for use as a leisure-time class activity.

I still have a scar on my knee from the last day of the fifth grade. I fell off my bicycle on the way home from school because I was trying to carry a couple of months' worth of art projects, unsuccessfully. My teacher was of the wait-to-take-it home school. Some artwork needs to be framed and spend some time hanging in the classroom, being decorative and inspirational. But children should be allowed to take some of their projects home immediately while they are still excited about them. It's good for morale.

Resources

BUTTON COLLECTING AND CRAFTING. Arden Newsome. New York: Lothrop, 1976. Everything you wanted to know but didn't think to ask about a very available craft medium—buttons!

CHILDREN'S CRAFTS. Compiled by the editors of *Sunset Magazine.* Menlo Park: Lane Publishing Company, 1976. A colorful, big-format paperback full of workable projects for kids.

Color Crafts Series: STRING, RAFFIA, AND MATERIAL (1971); *WORKING WITH PAPER* (1971); *CARD AND CARDBOARD* (1971); *WIRE, WOOD AND CORK* (1972); *PAINTING, PRINTING AND MODELING* (1972). New York: Franklin Watts. Big, colorful books which make use of simple materials for easy-to-hard projects—lots of them!

CONTEMPORARY AMERICAN FOLK ARTISTS. Elinor L. Horwitz. New York: Lippincott, 1975. An appealing collection of stories about and interviews with contemporary folk artists, many of them skilled in junk art. Photographs show some of the inventiveness and whimsy of these painters and sculptors.

DESIGNING WITH CUTOUTS: THE ART OF DECOUPAGE. Elyse Sommer. New York: Lothrop, 1973. Full of decoupage projects using cutouts, stamps, and photos.

FOLK TOYS AROUND THE WORLD AND HOW TO MAKE THEM. Joan Joseph. New York: Parents Magazine Press, 1972. Bullroarers, corn-cob donkeys, and shadow puppets are all illustrated in this beautiful little book. Many projects require some woodworking skill.

MAKING THINGS: THE HAND BOOK OF CREATIVE DISCOVERY. Ann Wiseman. Boston: Little, Brown and Co., 1973. Movie machines, quick clothes, conduit pipe xylophones, and other projects for kids using cheap and throwaway materials.

RECIPES FOR ART AND CRAFT MATERIALS. Helen Roney Sattler. New York: Lothrop, 1973. The best collection for art materials available. Includes pastes, modeling dough, casting compounds, paints, inks, fixes, and other money-saving materials.

RECYCLOPEDIA. Robin Simons. Boston: Houghton Mifflin, 1976. Crafts, games, and science projects, all using recycled materials. Ideas were developed at the Boston Children's Museum.

SIMPLE PRINTMAKING. Peter Weiss. New York: Lothrop, 1976. A handsome little book offering a variety of printing methods with throwaway materials.

SLOTTED SCULPTURE FROM CARDBOARD. Jeremy Comins. New York: Lothrop, 1977. Good ideas for slot sculptors (kids who like to use slits and slots for interconnecting parts).

SOCK CRAFT: TOYS, GIFTS, AND OTHER THINGS TO MAKE. Helen Roney Sattler. New York: Lothrop, 1972. Everything to do with old socks. Easy to read.

STEVE CANEY'S TOY BOOK. Steve Caney. New York: Workman, 1972. How-to-make-your-own old toys, new toys, and traditional folk toys with simple materials and tools.

WIZARD'S EYE. Charles Milligan and Jim Higgs. San Francisco: Chronicle Books, 1978. Not a project how-to book, but a good source of inspiration. Houses, energy, and furniture from junk.